PROTRACTED REFUGEE SITUATIONS:
Domestic and international security implications

GIL LOESCHER AND JAMES MILNER

ADELPHI PAPER 375

First published July 2005
by **Routledge**
4 Park Square, Milton Park, Abingdon, Oxon, OX14 4RN
for **The International Institute for Strategic Studies**
Arundel House, 13–15 Arundel Street, Temple Place, London, WC2R 3DX
www.iiss.org

Simultaneously published in the USA and Canada
by **Routledge**
270 Madison Ave., New York, NY 10016

Routledge is an imprint of the Taylor & Francis Group

© 2005 The International Institute for Strategic Studies

Director John Chipman
Editor Tim Huxley
Manager for Editorial Services Ayse Abdullah
Copy Editor Jill Dobson
Production Jesse Simon
Cover Photograph AFP/Getty

Typeset by Techset Composition Ltd, Salisbury, Wiltshire
Printed and bound in Great Britain by Bell & Bain Ltd, Thornliebank, Glasgow

British Library Cataloguing in Publication Data
A catalogue record for this book is available from the British Library

Library of Congress Cataloguing in Publication Data

ISBN 0-415-38298-X
ISSN 0567-932X

Contents

Index of maps, tables and figures

Glossary

AFRC	Armed Forces Revolutionary Council
ALCOP	All Liberian Coalition Party
ASEAN	Association of Southeast Asian States
AU	African Union
CIREFCA	International Conference on Central American Refugees
CPA	Comprehensive Plan of Action for Indochinese Refugees
DDRR	Disarmament, Demobilisation, Rehabilitation and Reintegration
DfID	Department for International Development
DKBN	Democratic Karen Buddhist Army
DPKO	Department of Peacekeeping Operations
DRC	Democratic Republic of Congo
ECOMOG	Economic Community of West African States Monitoring Group
ECOWAS	Economic Community of West African States
LAP	Local Assistance Project
LURD	Liberians United for Reconciliation and Democracy
NLD	National League for Democracy
ODP	Orderly Departure Program
RCMP	Royal Canadian Mounted Police
RPF	Rwandan Patriotic Front
RUF	Revolutionary United Front
SAARC	South Asian Association for Regional Cooperation
SLORC	State Law and Order Restoration Council
ULIMO-K	United Liberation Movement of Liberia for Democracy
UNDP	UN Development Programme
UNHCR	United Nations High Commissioner for Refugees
UN-OCHA	UN Office for the Coordination of Humanitarian Activities
UNOSOM	United Nations Operation in Somalia
UNRWA	United Nations Relief and Works Administration
UNSC	UN Security Council
UNSG	Office of the UN Secretary General
USAID	US Agency for International Development
WFP	World Food Programme

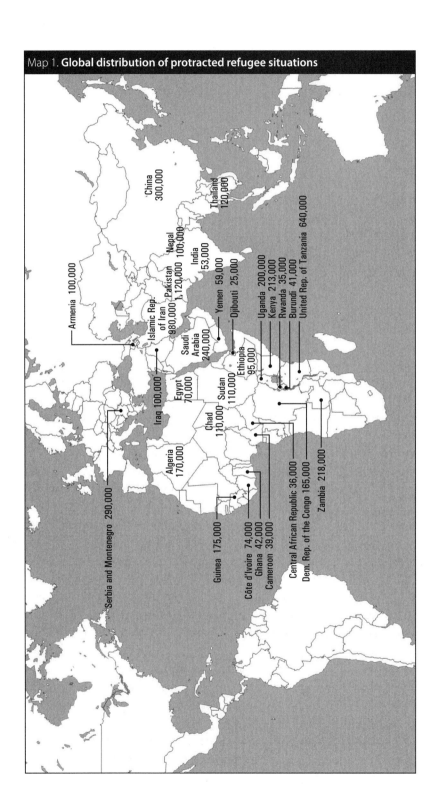

Map 1. Global distribution of protracted refugee situations

Armenia 100,000

China 300,000

Thailand 120,000

Nepal 100,000

Pakistan 1,120,000

India 53,000

Islamic Rep. of Iran 980,000

Yemen 59,000

Djibouti 25,000

Uganda 200,000

Kenya 213,000

Rwanda 35,000

Burundi 41,000

United Rep. of Tanzania 640,000

Saudi Arabia 240,000

Ethiopia 95,000

Egypt 70,000

Sudan 110,000

Iraq 100,000

Chad 110,000

Algeria 170,000

Serbia and Montenegro 290,000

Guinea 175,000

Côte d'Ivoire 74,000

Ghana 42,000

Cameroon 39,000

Central African Republic 36,000

Dem. Rep. of the Congo 165,000

Zambia 218,000

The significance of protracted refugee situations

Since the early 1990s, the United Nations and the international aid community have focused on refugee emergencies, delivering humanitarian assistance to refugees and war-affected populations, and encouraging large-scale repatriation programmes in high-profile regions such as the Balkans, the Great Lakes and, recently, Darfur and Chad. Almost two-thirds of the world's refugees, however, are trapped in protracted refugee situations. Such situations – often characterised by long periods of exile, stretching to decades for some groups – occur on most continents in a range of environments including camps, rural settlements and urban centres.

More recently, and especially since 11 September 2001, the United States and its allies have viewed international security policy through the prism of 'failing states', where a breakdown of institutions and governance has resulted in a vacuum of authority, leading to conditions where warlordism, terrorism and chronic instability flourish. A crucial but largely unrecognised component of peace-building processes in failing states in regions such as the Horn of Africa and West Africa is the relationship among chronic and recurring refugee flows, regional and intrastate conflict and economic underdevelopment. Recognising the link between the related problems of failed states and protracted refugee situations is an important first step in formulating an effective response to these sources of potential instability.

During recent years, donor governments and multilateral organisations have been inconsistent in their approaches to these chronic refugee situations. On the one hand, there is widespread recognition that recruitment into terrorist and rebel movements, the proliferation of small arms, the spill-over of civil conflict into neighbouring countries and the persistence of failed states are significant threats to international peace and security. On the other hand, Western donor governments have been reducing their engagement in the most chronic refugee situations, which are often closely related to many of these sources of insecurity. If Western security planners are serious about tackling many of the most pressing causes of insecurity, they must pay much closer attention to the resolution of protracted refugee situations.

Until 2001, the problem of protracted refugee situations was largely ignored by scholars and policymakers. While there has been some prelimi-nary discussion on the most prominent protracted refugee situations by UN and European Union (EU) policymakers, the focus of discussion has generally been on the humanitarian and economic implications of chronic refugee situations rather than the links between regional security and protracted refugee situations. To address these security issues, it is essen-tial to take into account the wider political and strategic contexts in which protracted refugee situations occur.

Political and security implications of protracted refugee situations

This Adelphi Paper addresses the neglected linkages in policy debate and research between protracted refugee situations and security. Long-term refugee populations are a critical element in ongoing conflict and instability, obstruct peace processes and undermine attempts at economic develop-ment. Recurring refugee flows are a source of international conflict: they generate instability in neighbouring countries and trigger interventions by host states and regional actors, and refugee camps can serve as bases and sanctuaries for armed groups that are sources of insurgency, resistance and terrorist movements. The militarisation of refugee camps creates a security problem for the country of origin, the host country and even internation-ally as graphically illustrated by the situation in Eastern Zaire/Democratic Republic of Congo (DRC) in 1994–96. Other security concerns, such as arms trafficking, drug smuggling, trafficking in women and children, and the recruitment of child soldiers and mercenaries, are known to occur in camps hosting protracted refugee situations.

The prolongation of refugee crises also has indirect security implications. Tensions between refugees and the local population often arise because refugees are perceived to receive preferential treatment, especially as access to local social services such as health and education become increasingly limited as a result of structural adjustment programmes and cut-backs in government spending while such services are widely available in the refugee camps through international aid programmes. As donor governments' engagement with camp-based refugee populations decreases over time, competition between refugees and the host population over scarce resources becomes a source of domestic tension and, potentially, instability. If assistance to the camps is reduced, some refugees may pursue coping strategies such as banditry, prostitution and petty theft, which become additional local security concerns.

In this way, protracted refugee situations are no less dangerous sources of instability than other more conventional security threats, and should be paid due attention by the US and other Western donor governments, relevant regional powers and multilateral security organisations. The outbreak of conflict and genocide in the Great Lakes Region of Central Africa in the early 1990s serves as a clear example of the potential implications of not finding solutions for long-standing refugee populations. Tutsi refugees who fled Rwanda between 1959 and 1962 and their descendants filled the ranks of the Rwandan Patriotic Front (RPF), which invaded Rwanda from Uganda in October 1990. Many of these refugees had been living in the sub-region for over 30 years. The Office of the United Nations High Commissioner for Refugees (UNHCR) acknowledged that 'the failure to address the problems of the Rwandan refugees in the 1960s contributed substantially to the cataclysmic violence of the 1990s'.[1] More than ten years after the 1994 genocide, it would appear that this lesson has yet to be learned, as dozens of protracted refugee situations remain unresolved in highly volatile and conflict-prone regions including the Horn of Africa, West Africa, the African Great Lakes, and South and Southeast Asia.

This lesson has not, however, been lost on those states that host prolonged refugee populations. In the wake of events in Central Africa, many host states, especially in Africa, increasingly view long-standing refugee populations as a security concern. These refugee populations are seen not as passive victims of persecution and conflict, but as active agents engaged in the politics not only of their country of origin but also in the host country and the wider region, and thus as a potential source of instability on a scale similar to that witnessed in Central Africa in the 1990s.

The political implications of protracted refugee situations are more fully understood in the context of the 'Third World security predicament' experienced by many states in Africa and Asia.[2] As highlighted in the work of Mohammed Ayoob and others, the nature of developing states and their peripheral place in the international system makes them especially vulnerable to external shocks. Given the regional dynamics of many conflicts in

Africa and Asia and the inability of states to insulate themselves effectively from the spill-over of conflict, the prolonged presence of refugees becomes an increasingly important political issue, both domestically and regionally.

These concerns are heightened as protracted refugee situations drop further down the political agenda of Western governments. 'Donor fatigue' has left many host states with fewer resources to address the needs of refugees and respond to the increased pressures on local environments and economies. According to the UNHCR, seven out of ten asylum seekers, refugees and others of concern to the agency are hosted in the world's poorest countries.[3] Given that these states are themselves heavily dependent on development aid to meet the needs of their own citizens, the additional burden of large refugee populations becomes all the more significant. In many host states, such concerns are often exacerbated by the additional pressures of democratisation and economic liberalisation, imposed through donor conditionality, and the rising expectations of local populations.

A third political implication of long-standing refugee populations is the strain that they often place on diplomatic relations between host states and the refugees' country of origin. The prolonged presence of Burundian refugees in Tanzania, coupled with allegations that anti-government rebels were based within the refugee camps, led to a significant breakdown in relations between the two African neighbours in 2000–02, to the point that the Burundian army shelled regions of Western Tanzania hosting large refugee populations. The prolonged presence of Burmese refugees on the Thai border has been a frequent source of tension between the governments in Bangkok and Rangoon. In a similar way, the elusiveness of a solution for the Bhutanese refugees in Nepal has been a source of regional tensions, drawing in not only the host state and the country of origin, but also India.

Many host states respond to these security and political concerns by containing refugees in isolated and insecure refugee camps, typically in remote border regions. Many host governments now require all refugees to live in designated camps, in contrast to earlier policies of permitting self-settlement of refugees, and place significant restrictions on refugees seeking to leave the camps, either for employment or educational purposes. This 'warehousing' of refugees[4] has significant human-rights and economic implications. As highlighted by the recent work of the US Committee for Refugees, sexual and physical violence in refugee camps is a significant concern. More generally, the prolonged encampment of refugee populations has led to the violation of a number of rights contained in the 1951 UN Convention Relating to the Status of Refugees, including freedom of movement and the right to seek wage-earning employment. Furthermore, containing refugees in camps makes them wholly dependent on international assistance, prevents them from pursuing economic self-reliance, and precludes them from contributing to the development of their host communities and states.[5] In cases where refugees have been allowed to engage in the local economy, it has been found that refugees can 'have a positive impact on the [local] economy by contributing to agricultural production, providing cheap labour and increasing local vendors' income from the sale of essential foodstuffs'.[6]

Overall, protracted refugee situations present significant and mounting challenges to security, human rights and development. Given the interaction between these concerns, the full significance of protracted refugee situations for host states in Africa and Asia becomes more apparent. There are also important political reasons for Western states to address protracted refugee situations. Apparently insoluble physical and economic insecurity has led large numbers of asylum seekers and migrants to move to Western countries, often using illegal means of entry, including smuggling and trafficking organisations. This has contributed to the asylum crisis in the West and has moved this issue high up the international political agenda. It is therefore very much in the national interest of Western policymakers to give greater priority to protracted refugee situations in regions of chronic instability.

Framework of the paper

Chapter one maps the numbers, scope and significance of protracted refugee situations, including an overview of contemporary cases, a working definition and a typology for their analysis. The chapter outlines the range of political, security, economic and humanitarian causes of protracted refugee situations both in the countries of refugee origin and in neighbouring host states, and concludes by arguing the current international policy responses are fragmented and crucially do not address the security implications of protracted refugee situations.

Chapter two traces the implications of forced migration over the past half-century for international relations. It argues that shifts in state attitudes toward sovereignty and intervention and state perceptions of internal and external threats to regime survival in the developing world have had a direct impact on international refugee policy. The chapter also provides an analytical framework for examining the security implications, both direct and indirect, of protracted refugee situations for regions in conflict and for host states.

Chapter three applies this analytical framework to some of the most prominent protracted refugee situations in Africa and Asia. The long-term presence of nearly 100,000 Liberians in Guinea, of 160,000 Somalis in

Kenya and of some 350,000 Burundians in Tanzania has come to be seen as security concerns by the host states and constitute a source of regional instability. In Southeast Asia, hundreds of thousands of Burmese have fled fighting inside Myanmar, forced village relocations, crop destruction and forced labour. More than 120,000 refugees (including Karen, Kareni, Mon and Shan) are confined in refugee camps inside Thailand. Others, including Burmese political dissidents, are urban refugees while approximately half a million illegal immigrants live in Thai towns and cities. The prolonged presence of Burmese refugees has significant implications for both Thai security as well as for regional cooperation and stability. In South Asia, more than 100,000 Bhutanese refugees have been restricted to refugee camps in Nepal since the early 1990s. The Lhotshampas are a source of regional tensions among Nepal, Bhutan and India and in recent years Maoist guerrillas have used the camps as recruiting grounds for their insurgency in Nepal and neighbouring Sikkim.

Chapter four provides a policy framework for devising comprehensive solutions that could more effectively address and even resolve protracted refugee situations. After examining past policy approaches to former protracted refugee situations and the likely benefits of these approaches to resolving current chronic situations, the chapter highlights both the essential preconditions and the elements of a comprehensive policy framework. There is a pressing need to develop a multilateral policy agenda that extends beyond conventional boundaries and seeks to integrate the resolution of chronic and recurring regional refugee problems with security, conflict resolution, capacity-building and economic development issues.

CHAPTER ONE

Defining the problem

Any examination of long-standing refugee populations in the developing world should begin with a definition of the nature and causes of protracted refugee situations.[1] Such a definition has remained elusive in recent years and this may have frustrated efforts to formulate effective policy responses. A more detailed understanding of the global scope and growing importance of the problem is also important as a basis for understanding the commonalities and differences of various protracted refugee situations, both contemporary and historical. The objective of this chapter is to provide analytical tools with which to examine protracted refugee situations.

Towards a working definition

UNHCR defines protracted refugee situation as,

> one in which refugees find themselves in a long-lasting and intractable state of limbo. Their lives may not be at risk, but their basic rights and essential economic, social and psychological needs remain unfulfilled after years in exile. A refugee in this situation is often unable to break free from enforced reliance on external assistance.[2]

In identifying the major protracted refugee situations in the world, UNHCR uses the 'crude measure of refugee populations of 25,000 persons or more who have been in exile for five or more years in developing countries'.[3]

This definition reinforces the popular image of protracted refugee situations as involving static, unchanging and passive populations and groups of refugees that are 'warehoused' in identified camps. In view of UNHCR's humanitarian mandate, and given the prevalence of encampment policies in the developing world, it should not be surprising that such situations have been the focus of UNHCR's engagement in the issue of protracted refugee situations. The UNHCR definition does not, however, fully encompass the realities of such situations. Far from being passive, recent cases illustrate how refugee populations have been engaged in identifying their own solutions, either through political and military activities in their countries of origin or through seeking means for onward migration to the West. In addition, evidence from Africa and Asia demonstrates that while total population numbers in protracted refugee situations remain relatively stable over time, there are, in fact, often significant changes within the membership of that population. For example, while the total number of Burundian refugees in Tanzania was relatively stable in recent years, at just under 500,000, there have been significant numbers of both new arrivals and repatriations to Burundi in recent years.

A more effective definition of protracted refugee situations would include not only the humanitarian elements proposed by UNHCR, but also a wider understanding of the political and strategic aspects of long-term refugee problems. Secondly, a definition should reflect the fact that protracted refugee situations also include chronic, unresolved and recurring refugee problems, not only static refugee populations. Thirdly, an effective definition must recognise that countries of origin, host countries and the international donor community are all implicated in long-term refugee situations.

Protracted refugee situations involve large refugee populations that are long standing, chronic or recurring. These populations are not static, often increasing and decreasing over time, and undergoing changes in composition. They are typically, but not necessarily, concentrated in a specific geographical area, but may include camp-based and urban refugee populations.[4] The nature of a chronic refugee situation will be influenced both by conditions in the refugees' country of origin and the responses and conditions in the host country. Refugees of one nationality in different host countries will result in different protracted refugee situations. For example, the circumstances of long-term Sudanese refugees in Uganda are different from those of Sudanese refugees in any of the other seven African host countries. In this way, one country may produce several protracted refugee situations.

Given the varied political causes and consequences of protracted refugee situations, it is difficult to lay down precise parameters of what size refugee population and how many years in exile constitute such a situation. Politically, the identification of a protracted refugee problem is, to a certain extent, the result of perception. If a refugee population is seen to have been in existence for a significant period of time without the prospect of resolution, then it may be termed a protracted refugee situation.

Trends in protracted refugee situations

Long-term refugee scenarios are a growing challenge. Not only are their consequences being more keenly felt by host states and regions of origin, but their total number has increased dramatically in the past decade. More significantly, protracted refugee problems now account for the vast majority of the global refugee population, demonstrating the importance, scale and global significance of the issue.

In the early 1990s, a number of long-standing refugee populations that had been displaced as a result of proxy wars in the developing world went home. In Southern Africa, huge numbers of Mozambicans, Namibians and others repatriated. In mainland southeast Asia, the Cambodians in exile in Thailand returned home and Vietnamese and Laotians were also repatriated. With the conclusion of conflicts in Central America, the vast majority of displaced Nicaraguans, Guatemalans and Salvadorans returned to their home countries. According to UNHCR, in 1993, in the midst of the resolution of these conflicts, there were 27 protracted refugee situations, with a total population of 7.9 million refugees.

While these Cold War conflicts were being resolved, and as refugee populations were being repatriated, new intra-state conflicts emerged and resulted in massive new refugee flows during the 1990s. Conflict and state collapse in Somalia, the African Great Lakes, Liberia and Sierra Leone generated millions of refugees. Millions more refugees were displaced as a consequence of ethnic and civil conflict in Iraq, the Balkans, the Caucasus and Central Asia. The global refugee population mushroomed in the early 1990s, and there was a pressing need to respond to the challenges of simultaneous mass influxes in many regions.

Ten years later, many of these conflicts and refugee situations remain unresolved. As a result, the number of long-term refugee populations is greater now than at the end of the Cold War. In 2003, there were 38 cases of refugee populations greater than 25,000 being in exile for five or more years, with a total protracted refugee population of 6.2m (see Table 1.1). While there are fewer long-staying refugees today, the number of chronic situations has greatly increased. In addition, refugees are spending longer periods of time in exile. It is estimated that 'the average of major refugee situations, protracted or not, has increased from nine years in 1993 to 17 years at the end of 2003'.[5] With a global refugee population of over 16.3m at the end of 1993, 48% of the world's refugees had been in exile for five or more years. At the end of 2003, the global refugee population stood at 9.6m, and over 64% of this number were in protracted refugee situations, usually in the most volatile regions.

It is also important to note that the percentage of the world's refugees in extended exile would increase significantly if the definition included groups of refugees smaller than 25,000. For example, such a definition would exclude the thousands of Liberian refugees in Ghana and Sierra Leone; Somalis in Djibouti, Eritrea and Tanzania; Burundians in the Democratic Republic of the Congo (DRC); and Burmese in Malaysia, to list but a few. It

Region / Country of asylum	Origin	UNHCR assistance status		Total	Percent Assisted
		Assisted[1]	Not assisted		
AFRICA		**1,600,000**	**620,000**	**2,300,000**	**70%**
Central Africa and Great Lakes		**670,000**	**370,000**	**1,000,000**	**67%**
Burundi	Dem. Rep. of the Congo	13,000	27,000	41,000	32%
Central African Rep.	Sudan	36,000	-	36,000	100%
Chad	Sudan	55,000	55,000	110,000	50%
Dem. Rep. of the Congo	Angola	43,000	81,000	120,000	36%
Dem. Rep. of the Congo	Sudan	11,000	34,000	45,000	24%
Rwanda	Dem. Rep. of the Congo	35,000	-	35,000	100%
United Rep. of Tanzania	Burundi	320,000	170,000	490,000	65%
United Rep. of Tanzania	Dem. Rep. of the Congo	150,000	-	150,000	100%
East and Horn of Africa		**620,000**	**55,000**	**670,000**	**93%**
Djibouti	Somalia	25,000	-	25,000	100%
Ethiopia	Sudan	95,000	-	95,000	100%
Kenya	Somalia	150,000	-	150,000	100%
Kenya	Sudan	63,000	-	63,000	100%
Sudan	Eritrea	73,000	35,000	110,000	66%
Uganda	Sudan	180,000	20,000	200,000	90%
Southern Africa		**130,000**	**91,000**	**220,000**	**59%**
Zambia	Angola	72,000	87,000	160,000	45%
Zambia	Dem. Rep. of the Congo	54,000	4,000	58,000	93%
West Africa		**220,000**	**110,000**	**330,000**	**67%**
Cameroon	Chad	-	39,000	39,000	0%
Côte d'Ivoire	Liberia	74,000	-	74,000	100%
Ghana	Liberia	42,000	-	42,000	100%
Guinea	Liberia	89,000	60,000	150,000	59%
Guinea	Sierra Leone	15,000	10,000	25,000	60%

Table 1. **Major Protracted Refugee Situations, as of 31 December 2003[6]**

would also be a larger figure if the calculation included elements of refugee population for whom a solution has been found for the majority of refugees. For example, the vast majority of some 200,000 Rohingya refugees from Myanmar who fled to Bangladesh in the early 1990s later repatriated. There remains, however, a group of some 20,000 Rohingya refugees in Bangladesh who continue to resist return. Such 'residual caseloads' constitute a considerable percentage of protracted refugee situations, but typically fall below the threshold of 25,000. However, as the case of the Rohingyas in Bangladesh, Rwandans in Uganda or Ghanaians in Togo clearly illustrate, these residual groups are among the most difficult to resolve. While the crude measure of 25,000 refugees in exile for five years should not be used as a basis for excluding other groups, it does provide a useful point of departure.

East and West Africa, South and Southeast Asia, the Caucasus, Central Asia, and the Middle East are all plagued with chronic refugee problems

Table 1 continued

Region / Country of asylum	Origin	UNHCR assistance status		Total	Percent Assisted
		Assisted	Not assisted		
CASWANAME[2]		2,300,000	420,000	2,700,000	85%
Algeria	Western Sahara	160,000	10,000	170,000	94%
Egypt	Occupied Palestinian Territory	-	70,000	70,000	0%
Iraq	Occupied Palestinian Territory	-	100,000	100,000	0%
Islamic Rep. of Iran	Afghanistan	830,000	-	830,000	100%
Islamic Rep. of Iran	Iraq	150,000	-	150,000	100%
Pakistan	Afghanistan	1,120,000	-	1,120,000	100%
Saudi Arabia	Occupied Palestinian Territory	-	240,000	240,000	0%
Yemen	Somalia	59,000	-	59,000	100%
ASIA AND THE PACIFIC		230,000	440,000	670,000	34%
China	Viet Nam	11,000	290,000	300,000	4%
India	China	-	92,000	92,000	0%
India	Sri Lanka	-	61,000	61,000	0%
Nepal	Bhutan	100,000	-	100,000	100%
Thailand	Myanmar	120,000	-	120,000	100%
EUROPE		340,000	190,000	530,000	64%
Armenia	Azerbaijan	50,000	190,000	240,000	21%
Serbia and Montenegro	Bosnia and Herzegovina	100,000	-	100,000	100%
Serbia and Montenegro	Croatia	190,000	-	190,000	100%
TOTAL		4,500,000	1,700,000	6,200,000	73%

[1] 'Assisted' refugees benefit from UNHCR's 'care and maintenance' programmes, typically receiving assistance in the form of food, shelter, health and education programmes. Such refugees also typically reside in government-designated zones, usually refugee camps.

[2] UNHCR's Regional Bureau for Central Asia, South West Asia, North Africa and the Middle East.

where refugees remain uprooted, unprotected and with no immediate prospect of a solution to their plight. Sub-Saharan Africa hosts the largest number of protracted refugee situations in one region: 22, involving a total of 2.3m refugees. The most important host countries on the continent are Tanzania, Kenya, Uganda, Zambia and Guinea. In contrast, the geographical area encompassing Central Asia, South West Asia, North Africa and the Middle East hosts eight major long-term populations, accounting for 2.7m refugees. The overwhelming majority are the Afghans in Pakistan and Iran, who total nearly 2m at the end of 2003. In Asia, there exist five protracted situations: a total of 670,000 refugees in China, Thailand, India and Nepal. In Europe, there were three major protracted populations, totalling 530,000 refugees, primarily in the Balkans and Armenia.

Causes of protracted refugee situations

As this overview illustrates, protracted refugee populations originate from the very states whose instability lies at the heart of chronic regional insecurity. The bulk of refugees in these regions – Somalis, Sudanese, Burundians, Liberians, Iraqis, Afghans and Burmese – come from countries where conflict and persecution have persisted for years. It is essential to recognise that protracted refugee situations have political causes, and therefore require more than humanitarian solutions. As argued by UNHCR,

> protracted refugee situations stem from political impasses. They are not inevitable, but are rather the result of political action and inaction, both in the country of origin (the persecution and violence that led to flight) and in the country of asylum. They endure because of ongoing problems in the country of origin, and stagnate and become protracted as a result of responses to refugee inflows, typically involving restrictions on refugee movement and employment possibilities, and confinement to camps.[7]

Protracted refugee problems are caused largely by both a lack of engagement by a range of peace and security actors in the conflict or human-rights violations in the country of origin, and a lack of donor government involvement with the host country. Failure to address the situation in the country of origin means that the refugee cannot return home. Failure to engage with the host country reinforces the perception of refugees as a burden and a security concern, which leads to encampment and a lack of local solutions. As a result of these failures, humanitarian agencies, such as UNHCR, are left to compensate for the inaction or failures of the major powers and the peace and security organs of the UN system.

To give one example, the extended presence of Somali refugees in East Africa and the Horn is the direct result of the consequences of failed intervention by the US and the UN in Somalia in the early 1990s and the inability or unwillingness of the major donor countries to engage in the task of rebuilding a failed state. As a result, hundreds of thousands of Somali refugees have been exiled within the region for over a decade, with humanitarian agencies like UNHCR and the World Food Programme (WFP) responsible for their care and maintenance as a result of increasingly restrictive host state policy.

In a similar way, failures on the part of the UN Security Council and regional organisations, such as the African Union (AU), the Economic Community of West African States (ECOWAS), the Association of Southeast Asian States (ASEAN) and the South Asian Association for Regional Cooperation (SAARC), to consolidate peace can lead to resurgence of conflict and displacement, leading to a recurrence of protracted refugee situations. For example, the return of Liberians from neighbouring West African states in the aftermath of the 1997 elections in Liberia was not sustainable. A renewal of conflict in late 1999 and early 2000 led not only to a suspension of repatriation of Liberian refugees from Guinea, Côte d'Ivoire and other states in the region, but led to a massive new refugee exodus. Following the departure into exile of Charles Taylor in 2003, there has been a renewed emphasis on return for the hundreds of thousands of Liberian refugees in the region, and large-scale facilitated repatriation began in late 2004. It does not, however, appear as though the lessons of the late 1990s have been learned. Donor support for demobilisation and reintegration of Liberian combatants has been limited, and there is rising concern over the possibility of a renewal of conflict, especially among former combatants who are again being recruited into rival factions.

The primary causes of protracted refugee situations are to be found in the failure of major powers, including the US and the EU, to engage in countries of origin and the failure to consolidate peace agreements. These examples also demonstrate how humanitarian programmes have to be underpinned by sustained political and security measures if they are to result in lasting solutions for refugees. Assistance to long-term refugee populations through humanitarian agencies is no substitute for sustained political and strategic action. More generally, the international donor community cannot expect the humanitarian agencies to respond to, let alone resolve, long-term refugee problems without the sustained engagement of the peace and security and development agencies, including the

UN Security Council, the UN Development Programme, the World Bank and related international, regional and national agencies.

Declining donor engagement in programmes to support long-standing refugee populations in host countries has also contributed to the rise in long-term refugee populations.[8] A marked decrease in financial contributions to assistance and protection programmes for chronic refugee groups has had not only security implications, as refugees and local populations compete for scarce resources, but has also reinforced host state perceptions of refugees as a burden. Host states now argue that the presence of refugees results in additional burdens on the environment, local services, infrastructure and the local economy, and that the international donor community is less willing to share this burden. As a result, host countries are less willing to engage in local solutions to protracted refugee situations, and more likely to contain refugees in isolated camps until a solution may be found outside the host country.

This trend first emerged in the mid-1990s, when UNHCR had budget shortfalls of tens of millions of dollars. These shortfalls were most acutely felt in Africa, where contributions to both development assistance and humanitarian programmes fell throughout the decade. There was also an apparent bias in the allocation of UNHCR's funding towards refugees in Europe over refugees in Africa. In 1999, it was reported that UNHCR spent about 11 cents per refugee per day in Africa, compared to an average of $1.23 per refugee per day in the Balkans.[9] In 2000 and 2001, most UNHCR programmes in Africa were forced to cut their budgets by 10–20%. Successive cut-backs to UNHCR's programme in Tanzania provide but one example. In 2001, the UNHCR was forced to reduce its budget in Tanzania by some 20%, resulting in the scaling-back of a number of activities.[10] In 2002, the UNHCR had to cut $2m from its total budget of $28m. Again, in 2003, UNHCR reported that it 'struggled to maintain a minimum level of health care, shelter and food assistance to the refugees in the face of reduced budgets'.[11] Similar shortages have affected food distribution in the camps. Dwindling support for the UN World Food Program (WFP) in Tanzania has reduced the food distributed to refugees on numerous occasions in recent years, most recently in November 2002 and again in February 2003, when the WFP was only able to distribute 50% of the normal ration, itself only 80% of the international minimum standard.[12]

Sensitive to these recurring shortfalls in donor support, the Tanzanian government has frequently stated that it is only willing to continue hosting refugees if it receives the necessary support from relevant international organisations. During the 1960s and 1970s, Tanzania was the vanguard of local settlement for refugees, distinguishing itself as only one of two African countries to grant mass naturalisation to refugees. In stark contrast, and in response to declining donor engagement, new Tanzanian regulations announced in 2003 now prohibit refugees from travelling more than 4km from the camps, a policy which greatly inhibits their access to wage-earning employment.

In this way, protracted refugee situations are caused by the combined effect of inaction or unsustained international action both in the country of origin and the country of asylum. These chronic and seemingly unresolvable problems occur because of ongoing political, ethnic and religious conflict in the countries of refugee origin and become protracted as a consequence of restrictions, intolerance and confinement to camps in host countries. Consequently, a truly comprehensive solution to protracted refugee situations must include sustained political, diplomatic, economic and humanitarian engagement in both the country of origin and the various countries of asylum. This engagement must begin by recognising the links between protracted refugee situations and host state and regional insecurity.

Chapter Two

Security implications of protracted refugee situations

Large refugee populations have always had important security implications. International political concern for refugees first emerged after
the First World War when mass flows from the break-up of the multi-
national Habsburg, Romanov, Ottoman and Hohenzollern empires in
Europe, Turkey and the Middle East and from the Russian Civil War,
the Russian–Polish War and the Soviet famine of 1921 heightened inter-
state tensions and threatened the security of European countries. These
refugee crises became protracted affairs that surpassed the capacity of
humanitarian agencies and individual states to resolve on their own.
Consequently, an international framework of institutions and agreements, a nascent international refugee regime, was created in 1921
within the League of Nations to deal with this contentious issue.[1]
Following the end of the Second World War, the current international
refugee regime emerged in reaction to the security threat posed to the
fragile European state system by some 12m displaced persons mainly
from Eastern and Central Europe and the Soviet Union.[2] While millions
of these refugees were either repatriated or resettled in the aftermath
of the Second World War, nearly 500,000 remained trapped in camps in
Western Europe until the mid-1960s.

While refugee movements were a central concern of both policymakers
and state actors throughout this period, the nature of their engagement
changed. This chapter argues that recognising the political and security
implications of refugee movements in the Cold War and post-Cold War

periods is an essential foundation for understanding the origins and significance of today's protracted refugee situations.

Refugees and security during the Cold War

During the Cold War, forced migration constituted one of the central concerns of US and Western foreign policies.[3] Refugees were seen as part of the global struggle between East and West. Refugees fleeing communism were portrayed as 'voting with their feet'. In the interest of exploiting the ideological and propaganda benefits of such movements, the West responded through generous burden-sharing and resettlement schemes. During the late 1970s and 1980s, the Indochinese exodus from and within Southeast Asia, the flow of Afghan refugees into Iran and Pakistan, the mass refugee outflows from Central America, the Angolan and Mozambican refugee populations in Southern Africa, and the Ethiopian and Sudanese refugee crises in the Horn of Africa all had significant security ramifications. In regions of intense superpower conflict and competition, refugees were armed and their military struggles were supported both materially and ideologically. Host states did raise security concerns about refugee flows, especially in the context of the Indochinese exodus from the late 1970s, but these concerns were comprehensively addressed by Western states in the interests of geostrategic priorities.

Throughout the Cold War, refugees and the security problems they raised were addressed as part of a broader and wider set of geo-political considerations and an understanding of security based on two major assumptions: that most threats to a state's security arose from outside its borders; and that these threats were primarily if not exclusively military in nature and required a political if not military response. Thus, while specific refugee groups were perceived as assets or liabilities in a number of Cold War crises, the logic of the Cold War was bound by a highly constrained notion of security which did not see migration as a central issue.

Security and refugees during the post-Cold War era

Since the early 1990s, a period of 'issue-widening', growing out of a frustration with the narrow Cold War understanding of security, emerged both in prominent security forums and in the literature. In particular, the security implications of forced migration gained new salience. As large-scale displacement of civilian populations became a deliberate conflict strategy in settings as diverse as the Balkans, sub-Saharan Africa and East Timor, it became clear that refugee movements were not only a consequence of insecurity, but could also be a cause of instability, for host states, for countries of origin, for regions in conflict and even a threat to wider international peace and security.

As intra-state conflicts broke out in the Middle East, the Balkans, the Caucasus, Africa and elsewhere, the security implications of refugee movements began to dominate political developments at the UN Security Council, NATO and other security forums. During this period, refugee issues were accorded a much higher place on the international security agenda, which created new opportunities for international action via the UN Security Council to respond to this problem, including the imposition of sanctions and military intervention against refugee-producing states.

Northern Iraq, Somalia, former Yugoslavia and Haiti saw UN-authorised international interventions in the domestic affairs of states in response to refugee flows. Following the end of the 1991 Gulf War, Iraqi suppression of widespread revolt in northern Kurdish areas created widespread fears among the Kurds, resulting in the mass flight of some 2m refugees to the Turkish border and into Iran. Civil war and famine in Somalia in 1991–92 displaced hundreds of thousands of civilians and caused large-scale starvation and a breakdown of civil order. The break-up of the former Yugoslavia in the early 1990s resulted in bitter civil wars among competing ethnic populations, including widespread ethnic cleansing and displacement. Human-rights abuses and repressive military rule drove large numbers of Haitians to flee the country by boat throughout the 1990s, causing a serious policy problem for the dominant regional power, the United States.

Forced displacements were at the centre of crises throughout the second half of the 1990s in the African Great Lakes region, Liberia, Sierra Leone, Albania, Kosovo, East Timor and Afghanistan. In Kosovo, over 850,000 people were driven out of the country in 1999 in a massive and brutal ethnic cleansing, providing the grounds for NATO intervention against Serbia. Later in the same year in the Indonesian-occupied territory of East Timor, gangs of armed thugs supported by the military and the police, waged a campaign of terror against the East Timorese people and against UN staff who were stationed there to monitor a referendum on the territory's future status.

As a consequence of these events during the past decade and a half, there has been increasing recognition that massive refugee flows may threaten international peace and security, and that they therefore may invoke the enforcement powers of the United Nations. As a potential threat to international peace and security, large refugee movements across borders may require not only humanitarian action, but a response under Chapter VII of the UN Charter, namely diplomatic action, the imposition of sanctions against the country of origin or even armed intervention to prevent the outflow of refugees or to facilitate their return. This link has been recognised for almost the past 20 years. As early as 1986, the report of a UN Group of Governmental Experts on International Cooperation to Avert New Flows of Refugees recognised the 'great political, economic and social burdens [of massive flows of refugees] upon the international community as a whole, with dire effects on developing countries, particularly those with limited resources of their own'.[4] Accordingly, it recommended intervention by the international community through the good offices of the Secretary-General, refugee prevention actions by appropriate UN bodies (including the Security Council), and better use of aid programs to deter massive displacements. The UN General Assembly subsequently endorsed the report, which explicitly defined such flows as a threat to peace and security, thus opening the door to action by the Security Council under Chapter VII several years later.

These arguments gained new momentum in the 1990s as conceptions of 'threats' and 'security' in interstate relations were reconsidered by the UN Security Council and a number of governments.[5] Certain internal acts and policies – including those triggering mass expulsions or refugee movements – were increasingly regarded as threats to others, particularly by their neighbours. From this perspective, grievous human-rights abuses became a matter of international concern when neighbouring states had to bear the cost of repression by having refugees forced upon them.[6] The Security Council itself took an increasingly inclusive view of 'threats to peace' where actual hostilities remained limited largely to the territory of a single state.[7] Indeed, in 1992, the UN Security Council's Summit Declaration included 'non-military sources of instability in the economic, social, humanitarian and ecological fields' as threats to international peace and security, while specifying the 'repatriation of refugees' alongside election monitoring and human-rights verification as an 'integral' part of the Security Council's efforts to maintain international peace and security'.[8]

At the same time that refugees came to be viewed as a possible source of threat to international and regional security (thus, in exceptional cases, providing a basis for action under Chapter VII of the UN Charter), states increasingly perceived refugees as burdens. In the face of growing numbers of illegal migrants and abuse of their asylum systems, Western governments, especially in Europe and North America, became increasingly reluctant in the early 1990s to grant asylum and enacted severe new entry controls.[9] The closure of borders to prevent unwanted refugee and migrant influxes became much more widespread than during the Cold War. In place of asylum, Western governments began to utilise various forms of 'temporary protection' to deal with those fleeing war and 'ethnic cleansing'. For developing countries too, growing numbers of displaced people presented problems for already precarious or failing economies that threatened domestic stability and central governmental authority. Diminishing donor government support for long-term refugee assistance, coupled with declining levels of development assistance, and the imposition by the international financial institutions of structural adjustment programmes on many poorer and less stable states, reinforced and contributed to many African and Asian governments' sense of vulnerability to external pressures and to their growing hostility towards refugees.

In response to these developments, the UN and major Western powers promoted a comprehensive policy which sought to modify the causes of refugee flows through conflict resolution, peacemaking and peacekeeping. These policies focused on unstable, refugee-producing regions, to facilitate the prevention, containment or reversal of refugee flows. This was achieved in the 1990s through a series of international humanitarian operations launched by the UN Security Council and the UNHCR. During this period, governments felt compelled to respond to refugee disasters, especially those covered by the media, and therefore repeatedly tasked humanitarian agencies, particularly the UNHCR, to provide emergency relief aid with a view towards alleviating, preventing or containing refugee movements within either the country or region of origin. For the world's most powerful states, providing humanitarian assistance was financially and politically a relatively low-risk option because it satisfied the demands of the media and public opinion for action to alleviate human suffering, and such assistance was often used as a substitute for dealing with the underlying political causes of refugee movements.[10]

Consequently, the UNHCR and other humanitarian agencies became involved more frequently in internal conflicts and in sharing responsibility with UN-mandated military forces for assisting displaced people.[11] In an effort to take advantage of the political opportunities that the post-Cold War environment presented, the UNHCR also made a concerted effort to frame its policies in terms of the major powers' interests in resolving conflicts and preventing refugee problems. By emphasising the responsibilities of refugee-sending states and by labelling the mass exodus of refugees as a threat to international security, UNHCR sought to legitimise its own facilitating of repatriations as well as interventions by the UN and states into regions of refugee origin to alleviate or even solve the causes of flight. The high priority given to humanitarian operations during the 1990s and the increasing recognition of a link between refugees and international security meant that UNHCR played an increasingly important role in placing refugees on the international political agenda. In 1992, Sadako Ogata, the High Commissioner for Refugees, began to report regularly to the Security Council and to regional organisations, such as the Organization for Security and Cooperation in Europe (OSCE) on the potentially destabilising effects of refugee and displacement crises.

The emergence of a new international security environment and a more assertive UN Security Council dramatically changed the way in which refugee problems were dealt with. During the Cold War, in-country assistance and protection of internally displaced people and victims of war were perceived by most governments to violate state sovereignty and were therefore taboo for UN agencies. In the post-Cold War period, by contrast, the UN responded experimentally to instances of forced displacement within internal conflicts. UN initiatives included the offer of temporary protection rather than full refugee status, the establishment of safe havens, cross-border delivery of assistance and the use of military resources to deliver assistance. For UNHCR, the major change in handling refugee issues included an increased focus on working in countries of origin – even in countries at war – to reduce the likelihood of massive refugee flows across borders. In addition, the UNHCR was also frequently asked by the UN Security Council and major donor governments to take part in comprehensive and integrated UN peacekeeping or peacemaking operations.

'Issue-widening' in the field of security studies

In tandem with policy developments in the conduct of international politics and security during the 1990s, international relations analysts began to broaden their conceptualisation of security. Policy researchers highlighted how migration and refugee movements, as well as environmental degradation, economic interdependence and transnational crime had the potential to influence state and regional security agendas.[12] Consequently, new thinking on the links between refugee movements and international security emerged.

In the early post-Cold War period, think-tanks and universities alike took cognisance of the rising importance of security in migration and refugee studies. Works by Gil Loescher and Myron Weiner drew attention to forced migration as both a potential cause and consequence of insecurity, emphasising its 'high politics' dimensions and charting a cross-regional framework for future research.[13] They argued that it was essential to recognise that refugee problems are intensely political problems with the potential to create domestic instability, generate interstate tension, and threaten regional and sometimes international security, and argued that solutions needed political as well as humanitarian dimensions.[14]

These early studies aimed to provide a basic typology of migration flows and their related security concerns, particularly for sending and receiving states. Particular reference was also made to the numerous cases of 'refugee warriors'[15] and their negative impact on regional and international security. However, these early works did not incorporate a comprehensive conceptualisation of 'security' appropriate to the experiences and pressures facing many developing-world host states. While attempting to bring the migration question into the security studies mainstream, the focus was disproportionately on the 'high politics' dimension of the security concerns of host-states at the expense of the 'low politics' concerns. As recent cases illustrate, the domestic, 'low politics', or indirect security concerns, have proven to be far more pervasive and preoccupying for host states than previously thought, especially in Africa and parts of Asia.

From the mid-1990s, writings on migration and security focused more on the securitisation of asylum in the European context.[16] The debate focused on the way that societal identity and societal concerns about asylum and immigration translate into state action against asylum seekers and migrants. These concerns have been heightened since the terrorist attacks in the United States on 11 September 2001 and the subsequent US-led 'global war on terror'. The new security agenda has sharpened the association, for many Western analysts, between refugees, asylum seekers and illegal migrants on the one hand, and insecurity on the other. During the current decade, there has been an emphasis on the potential links between migration and asylum in the West and transnational crime, terrorism, national identity and societal security.[17] As a result of these concerns, many Western countries have reconsidered their procedures for admitting refugees. In the EU, improving the management of the porous borders of adjoining regions and controlling illegal migration and trafficking has become a priority for policymakers.[18]

Many Western policymakers are increasingly of the view that the potential security implications of refugee movements can be contained in regions of refugee origin. This approach, combined with efforts to find ways to avoid the 'secondary movement' of refugees from countries of first asylum to Europe and North America, has encouraged Western policymakers (especially in the UK, Denmark and the Netherlands) to consider seriously 'regional processing' and 'zones of protection'. However, 'regionalisation' may increase the burdens borne by host states, compound their security concerns and increase their reluctance to host refugees.[19]

Mohammed Ayoob's definition of security for developing countries provides an appropriate framework to discuss the nature of threats posed by protracted refugee situations to many governments in Africa and Asia today:

> Security or insecurity is defined in relation to vulnerabilities, both internal and external, that threaten to, or have the potential to bring down or significantly weaken state structures, both territorial and institutional, and regimes.[20]

In Ayoob's view, regime security in relation to state-making is of fundamental importance in developing countries, particularly in countries with poor governance, economic weakness, porous borders and hostile relations with neighbouring states. Protracted refugee situations exacerbate these vulnerabilities in many host states.

The prolongation of refugee crises has become a significant political issue both domestically and regionally for many African and Asian host states. Ill-defined, porous borders make it difficult for states to protect themselves from the spill-over of refugees fleeing conflict in neighbouring countries. The long-term presence of large concentrations of refugees exacerbates other security concerns such as arms-trafficking, drug-smuggling, the recruitment of soldiers, and the trafficking of women and children, over which many host governments have little control. These security concerns are magnified when refugee influxes evolve into long-term refugee populations and when the major donor governments lose political interest and fail to provide sufficient assistance. Thus, host states perceive protracted refugee situations as posing direct and indirect threats to their security and regime survival.

Direct threats

The direct threats faced by the host-state, posed by the spill-over of conflict and the presence of 'refugee warriors', are by far the strongest link between refugees and conflict. Here, there are no intervening variables between forced migration and violence as the migrants themselves are actively engaged in armed campaigns often, but not exclusively, against the country of origin. Such campaigns have the potential of regionalising the conflict and dragging the host-state into what was previously an intra-state conflict. Such communities played significant roles in regionalising conflict in Africa and Asia during the Cold War. With the end of the Cold War, the logic has changed, but the relevance of refugee warriors remains. This relevance was brought home with particular force in the maelstrom of violence that gripped the Great Lakes region of Central Africa between 1994 and 1996.

The direct causes of insecurity for both host states and regional and extra-regional actors stemming from chronic refugee populations are best understood within the context of so-called failed states, as in Somalia, and the rise of warlordism, as in the case of Liberia. In such situations, refugee camps are used as bases for guerrilla, insurgent or terrorist activities. Armed groups hide behind the humanitarian character of refugee settlements, using them to recruit among disaffected displaced populations. In such situations, there is the risk that humanitarian aid, including food, medical assistance and other support mechanisms, may be expropriated to support armed elements.[21] From camps, some refugees continue their activities and networks that support armed conflicts in their home country. Similar security concerns may arise within urban refugee populations where gangs and criminal networks can emerge within displaced and disenfranchised populations. These groups take advantage of the transnational nature of refugee populations, of remittances from abroad and the marginal existence of urban refugees to further their goals. In both the urban and camp context, refugee populations have provided a cover for illicit activities, ranging from prostitution and people-smuggling to trade in small arms, narcotics and diamonds. Such activities are prominent characteristics commonly associated with the long-standing Burmese refugee population in Thailand and the Liberian refugees throughout West Africa.

The security consequences of such activities for host states and regional actors are tangible.[22] They include cross-border attacks on both host states and countries of origin, attacks on humanitarian personnel, refugees and civilian populations. Direct security concerns can also lead to serious bilateral and regional political and diplomatic tensions. Host states perceive cross-border refugee flows as impinging on their national sovereignty, especially given the tenuous control that many central governments in the developing world have over their border regions. Finally, the activities of armed elements among refugee populations not only violate refugee protection and human rights principles, but may constitute threats to international peace and security. For example, the training and arming of the Taliban in the refugee camps in Pakistan during the 1980s and 1990s underscores the potential threat to regional and international security posed by refugee warriors.

In East Africa, both Kenya and Tanzania have raised significant concerns about the direct security threat posed by long-standing refugee populations fleeing from neighbouring countries' wars. In particular, Kenya feels vulnerable to the spill-over of conflict from neighbouring states and from terrorist activities. Kenya's porous borders and its position as a regional diplomatic and commercial centre made it a target of international terrorist attacks in 1998 and 2002. Kenya is also concerned about the flow of small arms into its territory, especially its urban areas, primarily from Somalia. As a result of the links between Islamic fundamentalism, the lack of central authority in Somalia and a long history of irredentism within its own ethnic Somali population, the government in Nairobi now views Somali refugees on its territory almost exclusively through a security prism.

The presence of armed elements in western Tanzania and allegations that the refugee camps serve as a political and military base for Burundian rebel groups have been the source of significant security concerns for the government in Dar-es-Salaam. Tensions deriving from these allegations have led to open hostilities between Tanzania and Burundi, including the exchange of mortar fire across the border. Concerns have also been raised by politicians and police about the perceived rise in urban gun crime resulting from the flow of small arms from Burundi. Consequently, the Tanzanian government has increased restrictions on Burundian refugees, is pushing for early repatriation, and has also adopted the official policy that refugees should be restricted to safe havens in their country of origin.

Indirect threats

More difficult to identify, but just as potentially destabilising as direct threats, are the indirect threats that refugee movements may pose to the host state. Indirect threats may arise when the presence of refugees causes grievances among local populations. At the root of such problems, often, is the failure of international solidarity and burden-sharing with host countries. Local and national grievances are particularly heightened when refugees compete with local populations for resources, jobs and social services, including health care, education and housing.[23] Refugees are sometimes seen as a privileged group in terms of services and welfare provisions, especially where such services are not available to the local population, or as the cause of low wages in the local economy and inflation in local markets. Refugees are also frequently scapegoats for breakdowns in law and order in both rural and urban refugee populated areas.

The mass arrival and prolonged presence of refugees may also exacerbate previously existing inter-communal tensions in the host country and shift the balance of power between communities within a host state. In this sense, it has been argued that 'in countries which are divided into antagonistic racial, ethnic, religious or other groupings, a major influx can place precariously balanced multi-ethnic societies under great strain and may even threaten the political balance of power'.[24] In this way, the presence of refugees has been demonstrated to exacerbate that host country's 'existing internal conflicts'.[25] This concern was explicit in Macedonia's reluctance to accept Kosovar Albanian refugees in March 1999, because they 'threatened to destabilise Macedonia's ethnic balance'.[26] Other examples include the arrival of Iraqi Kurds in Turkey, of Afghan Sunni Muslims in Shia-dominated Pakistan, or of Pashtun Afghans in the Baluchi-dominated Pakistani region of Baluchistan.[27]

However, not all refugees are seen as threats. The question of which refugees are seen as threats, and why, may be partially explained by whether or not refugees are accepted as members of the local community. Indeed,

> 'in the Third World, the remarkable receptivity provided to millions of Afghans in Pakistan and Iran, to ethnic kin from Bulgaria in Turkey, to Ethiopians in the Sudan, to Ogadeni Ethiopians in Somalia, to southern Sudanese in Uganda, to Issaq Somali in Djibouti and to Mozambicans in Malawi has been facilitated by the ethnic and linguistic characteristics they share with their hosts'.[28]

In this sense, the importance of ethnic and religious affinity cannot be overstated. If a host community perceives the incoming refugee as 'one of us', then positive and generous conceptions of distributive justice will apply.

Conversely, if refugees are seen as members of an 'out-group', they are likely to receive a hostile reception. In cases where there is a division along ethnic, linguistic or religious lines, 'a major population influx can place precariously balanced multi-ethnic societies under great strain and may even threaten the political balance of power'.[29] Indeed, refugees, 'as an out-group, can be blamed for all untoward activities'.[30] One southern African researcher argues that the 'presence of massive numbers of refugees' can 'create feelings of resentment and suspicion, as the refugee population increasingly, and often wrongly, gets blamed for the economic conditions that may arise within the domestic population'.[31] This can lead to a point where 'poverty, unemployment, scarcity of resources, and even crime and disease, are suddenly attributed to the presence of these refugees and other foreigners'.[32] The growing xenophobia in many African countries, often resulting from rapid democratization and other pressures, is a key factor motivating restrictive asylum policies in the past decade. With the growth of democracy on the continent, 'governments are compelled to take into account public opinion in formulating various policies. The result has been the adoption of anti-refugee platforms by political parties which result in anti-refugee policies and actions by governments'.[32] Just as politicians in Western Europe faced increasing pressures to restrict entry as asylum became a significant issue in domestic politics, in recent years 'the rise of multiparty democracy in Africa ... has arguably diminished the autonomy of state elites in determining the security agenda'.[33]

Due consideration of the indirect threat to security that long-staying refugees may pose to host states has been lacking in both the research on and policy towards refugee movements. In these cases, it is not the refugee that is a threat to the host state, but the context within which the refugees exist that results in the securitisation of the asylum question for many states. Lacking policy alternatives, many host governments now present refugee populations as security threats to justify actions that would not otherwise be permissible, such as denying refugees freedom of movement, preventing new arrivals of refugees and, in exceptional circumstances, carrying out mass expulsions. As argued above, these pressures arise especially when the state is confronted with the pressures of externally promoted democratisation and economic liberalisation. A prominent example of this phenomenon was the Tanzanian government's decision in March 1995 to close the border with Burundi to prevent the arrival of additional refugees and the role this decision played in the run-up to the country's first multiparty elections.[34]

This chapter has attempted to clarify the complex relationship between protracted refugee situations and host state and regional security and to develop an analytical framework to understand better the nature of direct and indirect security concerns that protracted refugee situations pose to many host governments and societies in the developing world. The next chapter will apply this analytical framework to some of the most prominent protracted refugee situations in Africa and Asia.

CHAPTER THREE

Case studies: contemporary protracted refugee populations in Africa and Asia

This chapter critically examines the refugee-related security concerns of several states in Africa and Asia that host large protracted refugee populations. It focuses on the current political, economic and security factors involved in the Bhutanese, Burmese, Burundian, Liberian and Somali long-term refugee problems in the host states of Nepal, Thailand, Tanzania, Guinea and Kenya as well as on the interests of external key actors. The objective in examining these cases is to develop a deeper understanding of both the direct security burden, including the presence of armed elements within the refugee populations and the spill-over of conflict across borders, and of the indirect security burden, particularly the exacerbation of previously existing tensions in the host communities. Finally, the chapter assesses the relevance and applicability of past and current policy efforts in dealing with contemporary chronic refugee problems.

The most visible and long-standing protracted refugee situation in the world today is that of the Palestinians. The original Palestinian displacement occurred in 1948 when 700,000 Palestinians fled their homes during the conflict that accompanied the creation of Israel. In 1949 a UN General Assembly resolution established a special international institution, the United Nations Relief and Works Administration (UNRWA), to assist Palestinian refugees.[1] UNRWA's specific mandate was to provide emergency assistance, not political or legal protection, to Palestinians displaced by war. A year later, UNHCR was created with a mandate to provide legal protection to all other refugees in the world. Thus, from the inception of this protracted refugee problem, Palestinians were excluded from the protection of the international refugee regime, treated as a special case and regarded as a separate political problem. UNRWA began operations throughout the Middle East in 1951 and continues to function today. Currently, there are some 6m Palestinian exiles, just over 4m of whom are registered as refugees with UNRWA.

A less well-known or politically visible chronic refugee situation is that of the 170,000 Saharawis who have lived in extended exile in refugee camps near Tindouf in Western Algeria for the past 30 years. The Saharawi fled the former Western Sahara in 1975 after Morocco forcibly annexed the territory following the departure of the Spanish colonial government. During the past three decades, the Saharawis, with the support of the Algerian government, have waged armed resistance to Moroccan rule.[2] The Saharawi military arm, the Polisario Front, has used the camps at Tindouf as a base from which to organise its political struggle and to recruit its soldiers.

Both the Palestinian and the Saharawi refugees share many similarities with other protracted refugee situations throughout the world. When wars persist for decades, refugees remain in limbo with no firm place of residence. They are largely confined to refugee camps or settlements, have little or no livelihood and are highly dependent on international assistance. Prolonged and unresolved refugee crises almost universally result in politicisation and militancy of refugee communities with predictable adverse consequences for host state and regional security. These populations frequently become the archetypal 'refugee warrior' communities.

However, there are also important differences between the Palestinian and Saharawis and other protracted refugee situations across the globe. Unlike most chronic refugee problems in Africa and Asia, the Palestinians remain firmly at the centre of international political attention and engage the geopolitical interest of the United States and other major powers. While the root causes of the Palestinian–Israeli conflict are much debated, nearly everyone agrees that a sustainable peace in Israel and the Middle East requires a solution to the problem of Palestinian refugees. Atypically, the Saharawi refugee problem is a direct consequence of the peculiarities of the Spanish colonial withdrawal from Western Sahara and its subsequent annexation by Morocco 30 years ago. Despite a UN initiative in the early 1990s to hold a referendum among the population of Western Sahara to decide their future, no vote has yet occurred. Thus, one of the longest-running protracted refugee situations remains deadlocked, with Morocco refusing to accommodate Saharawi interests and Algeria using the Polisario Front as a proxy to check Morocco's regional ambitions. Both the Palestinians and Saharawi, therefore, are highly specific cases stemming from particular historical and political factors that are not replicated elsewhere.

Most of the protracted refugee situations investigated here first emerged in the immediate aftermath of the Cold War and have remained unresolved. They stagnate in the context of failed states, as in Somalia, and the rise of warlordism, as in the case of Liberia. They are the result of political inaction, and neglect of the likely resurgence of ethnic conflict and genocide, as in Burundi and Rwanda. These examples are stalemated because of the international failure to take action in response to either acts of ethnic cleansing, as in Bhutan, or the systematic human-rights violations of authoritarian and military regimes, as in Myanmar.

These refugee crises have become protracted because of political impasses both in the country of origin and in the country of asylum. The persecution or violence and domestic threats to regime survival that led to refugee flight in most of these source countries over a decade ago persist today, making repatriation difficult if not impossible. Host countries, because of their internal and external vulnerabilities and lack of societal cohesion and state legitimacy, perceive long-staying refugee populations as security concerns. Consequently, they impose restrictions on refugees, confining them to camps and refusing employment and local integration possibilities.

Perhaps most importantly, these conflicts do not directly impinge upon the post-Cold War interests of the major powers and therefore remain largely unaddressed internationally. While, in some cases, especially in the case of the Great Lakes during the mid-1990s, massive displacement resulted in unprecedented international humanitarian engagement, this action was not coupled with political or strategic engagement, and has not been sustained since the end of the emergency phases of these conflicts. Hence conflicts are either not resolved or recur, leading to renewed outflows of refugees and the prolongation of the problem for neighbouring states. While there has been some progress in responding to the short-term security implications of protracted refugee situations, especially in Africa,[3] there have been virtually no significant policy initiatives on resolving the underlying causes of conflict and displacement. As long as humanitarian efforts are not coupled with sustained political, economic and security initiatives, these populations will remain a potential source of regional insecurity.

The focus here is on five cases in sub-Saharan Africa and in South and Southeast Asia that involve issues common to the majority of protracted refugee situations today. The cases of the Somalis in Kenya, Liberians in Guinea, Burundians in Tanzania, the Bhutanese in Nepal and the Burmese in Thailand demonstrate how long-term refugee populations can result in both direct and indirect security consequences for host states and countries of origin in conflict-prone and so-called 'failed' regions.

Refugees from Somalia in Kenya

Prior to the mass influx of refugees from Somalia in the 1990s, Kenya hosted a relatively small refugee population. The situation changed dramatically with the arrival in Kenya in 1991–92 of over 400,000 refugees from Somalia, fleeing civil war, famine and state collapse. Both the mass arrival of refugees and their prolonged presence have confronted Kenya with a number of direct and indirect security concerns.

The root causes of the Somali displacement are to be found in the collapse of the Somali state in the early 1990s, the withdrawal of international engagement in the mid-1990s, and a decade of stagnation and international neglect.[4] Violence aimed at the overthrow of the regime of Said Barre began in Somalia in 1988, but quickly descended into civil war. By late 1990, the government no longer had control outside Mogadishu as dozens of militant and political groups, mostly based on the Somali clan system, established pockets of influence throughout Somalia. Fighting erupted in the capital in November and central authority in Somalia collapsed on 27 January 1991, when Said Barre and his regime fled Mogadishu. Factional violence filled the power vacuum.

The combined effects of the fighting, famine and anarchy led to an increasingly complex emergency. 800,000 refugees had fled Somalia by the end of 1992, while well over one million became internally displaced. About half of the refugees leaving Somalia fled to Kenya, where the number of refugees rose from 39,000 in July 1991 to 92,200 by December 1991. The rate of arrivals continued to climb the following year, with the refugee population in Kenya reaching an estimated 246,000 in May 1992 and peaking at 427,278 by the end of 1992.

In April 1992, the UN Security Council passed Resolution 794, stating that the 'magnitude of human suffering in Somalia' constituted a threat to international peace and security and authorising the deployment of an additional 3,500 personnel of the United Nations Operation in Somalia (UNOSOM) to help ensure the safety of humanitarian personnel in Somalia. In addition, the Security Council, acting under Chapter VII of the UN Charter, authorised the use of 'all necessary means to establish as soon as possible a secure environment for humanitarian relief operations in Somalia'.[5]

The deployment of UNOSOM, however, had only a minimal impact on the security situation in Somalia. This insecurity seriously limited the response to the 1992 famine, which killed an estimated 300,000 Somalis.

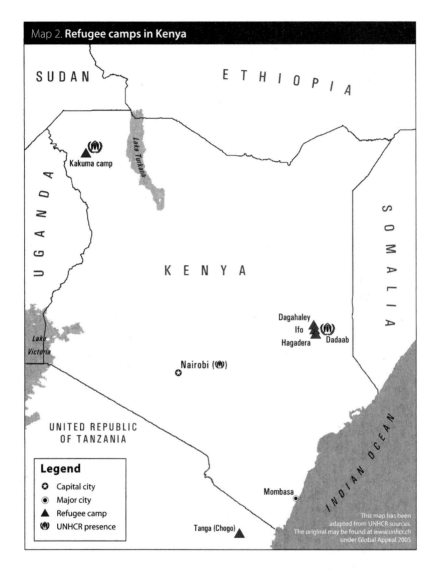

Map 2. **Refugee camps in Kenya**

Aid agencies operating throughout the country increasingly came under attack by local militias. This situation prompted the US government to deploy troops to Somalia in December 1992 under *Operation Restore Hope*. US engagement was, however, short-lived. In the aftermath of a failed US military operation on 3 October 1993 to capture militia leader General Aideed in Mogadishu, President Bill Clinton withdrew American troops from Somalia in March 1994. UN troops departed shortly thereafter.

Ten years after the withdrawal of the last foreign troops, Somalia is a failed state without a central government. As a result, there has been little change in the Somali refugee population in Kenya. Following short-lived humanitarian efforts in 1993, the refugee population dropped below 200,000 in 1994, and has ranged between 141,000 and 172,000 in the last ten years. In 2003, UNHCR reported that there were just over 154,000 Somali refugees in Kenya, making it by far the largest refugee population in the country.[6] Given the lack of solutions in Somalia and the general reluctance of Western countries to resettle Somali refugees, coupled with Kenya's rejection of the possibility of local integration, the Somali refugee population is also the most protracted of the ten refugee populations hosted in Kenya.

This stabilisation in the number of refugees in the mid-1990s was not, however, mirrored in the stabilisation of their security. The majority of the refugees were housed in several camps in the extreme northeast of Kenya. The location of the camps, just a few miles from the Kenya–Somali border, significantly compromised the security of refugees. Bandits, collectively referred to as *shiftas,* attacked seemingly at will, targeting the camps in search of food and money. Refugee women and girls were especially victims of this rise in insecurity with an alarming number of them falling victim to rape by Kenyan and Somali bandits while outside the camps foraging for firewood.[7] It soon became clear that humanitarian efforts in Somalia and the short-lived international intervention simply displaced the warring groups into Kenya, resulting in a spill-over of the violence. With the withdrawal of the US and UN presence from Somalia, a vacuum of authority was created that further allowed the *shiftas* free rein to continue their activities.

From the moment of their arrival, the Kenyan government identified Somali refugees as a security concern. The challenge of responding to the refugees was compounded by a number of other pressures on President Daniel arap Moi's weakening regime: pressure from the international donor community, who suspended aid in November 1991 pending democratisation and improved governance; and domestic pressure as a result of pre-election 'land clashes', which involved attacks on pro-opposition Kikuyu farms in the Western and Rift Valley Provinces of Kenya by pro-government Kalenjin youths and resulted in the internal displacement of an estimated 300,000 Kenyans.[8]

Confronted with these multiple challenges, the government pursued a dual policy towards refugees. Kenya opened its borders and allowed hundreds of thousands of refugees to enter, a move that won praise from the international donor community. In response to its security concerns, however, the government closed the few secure camps that were close to urban areas, especially Nairobi and Mombasa.[9] Refugees from these camps were either forced to go home or were transferred to the more violent and insecure camps in the northeast, on the political and physical periphery of the state.[10] To reinforce this encampment policy, since 1996 the police have conducted regular raids in urban areas to apprehend refugees found living illegally outside the camps.[11]

Through a range of public statements and in private interviews, the Kenyan government continues to highlight a range of security concerns relating to the prolonged presence of Somali refugees. At the national level, there is a perception that the presence of Somali refugees has resulted in direct security threats to the Kenyan state and the governing regime.[12] These direct threats relate to the flow of small arms into Kenya and the threat of terrorism, exacerbated by its long and porous border with Somalia. As a result of these perceived threats, the Kenyan state has viewed the Somali refugee population as a security concern, thereby reinforcing Nairobi's longstanding policy of requiring Somali refugees to reside in the isolated and insecure Dadaab refugee camps.[13]

Kenya has been the target of at least two major terrorist attacks in recent years. In early August 1998, the US Embassy in central Nairobi was attacked by a car bomb. Over 250 people were killed, and some 5,000 injured, most of them Kenyans. On 28 November 2002, in the run-up to the presidential elections, coordinated attacks took place in Mombasa, Kenya's second largest city. Almost simultaneously, three suicide bombers attacked the Paradise Hotel, killing 16, while two surface-to-air missiles narrowly missed their target of an Israeli charter plane during take-off. US and Kenyan investigators have blamed both the 1998 and the 2002 attacks on Somali-based Islamic organisations with links to the al-Qaeda network. Shortly after the Mombasa attacks, US intelligence sources reportedly blamed a group known as al-Ittihad al-Islamiya, 'a prominent militant group in the Horn of Africa with links to Osama bin Laden's al-Qaeda network',[14] for the attacks.

Kenyan and US investigations into the activities of al-Ittihad al-Islamiya eventually led to the Dadaab refugee camps. Investigators believed that Kenya's porous border with Somalia and the presence of refugee camps provided the ideal cover for the operations of a terrorist organization, while the disaffected camp population provided a fertile base for recruitment.[15] It was also believed that there was a direct link between al-Ittihad al-Islamiya and the Saudi-based al-Haramain Islamic Foundation, which provided some religious training in the camps and donated food during Ramadan.[16] In March 2002, the US Treasury Department had blocked the funds of the Somalia branch of al-Haramain, claiming that was linked to al-Ittihad al-Islamiya, itself closely linked to the al-Qaeda network.[17] As a result, a connection, albeit tenuous, has been drawn between the terrorist attacks on Kenya and the presence of refugees.

Likewise, a connection has been drawn between the presence of refugees and the flow of small arms into Kenya, where the availability of such weapons has increased dramatically, serving 'to intensify deadly bandit attacks and clan rivalries' in the country's northeast.[18] As a result of the increased insecurity, more people are arming themselves, thus fuelling the spiral of violence, which has now spread into Nairobi. For many in the government, the rise in gun crime in Nairobi is a direct result of Somali refugees bringing weapons into the country.

A long history of conflict between the Kenyan state and ethnic Somalis living in Kenya, resulting from the *shifta* wars of the 1960s and the 30-year state of emergency in Kenya's North Eastern Province, has reinforced the image of all Somalis as a source of insecurity.[19] However, the flow of small arms into Kenya is facilitated by the lack of central authority in Somalia, not primarily by the refugees. Likewise, no substantive proof has emerged as to the links between terrorism and the camps. In the public view, however, everyone crossing the border from Somalia is a refugee. It is on the basis of this association, and the fact that terrorism in the region and small arms proliferation do have roots in Somalia, that Somali refugees are perceived as direct security threats by the Kenyan government.

The indirect security issues relating to the protracted presence of the Somali refugees are of much greater concern to Nairobi. These include conflict between refugees and the local population resulting from competition over scarce resources, which is exacerbated by diminishing support to the camps, and levels of banditry and violent crime in and around the camps.

The Dadaab camps are located in a semi-arid region of Kenya where 'conflict over resources between a number of local Ogadeni clans was a feature … prior to the arrival of the refugees in the 1990s'.[20] Already delicate clan relations were challenged, and the potential for conflict increased, by the arrival of the refugees, who 'brought to the area and the refugee camps a history of clan rivalries from Somalia.'[21]

There has also been a dramatic rise in the grievances, exploited by local politicians, felt by the local population towards the refugees. Given that in the camps, refugees have access to free health care and education, as well as other services not provided to the Kenyan population, the host community perceives the refugees as a privileged group. Many also see the refugees as a threat to the region's fragile economy. When combined with the chronic and acute resource-scarcity characteristic of the area around Dadaab, it is easy to see how this has led to conflict.

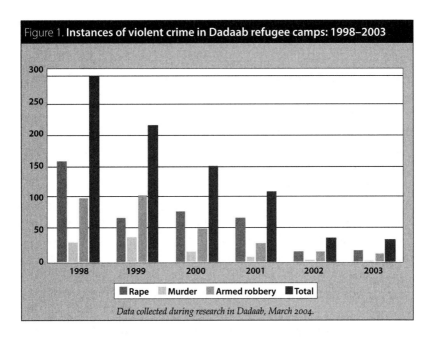

Figure 1. **Instances of violent crime in Dadaab refugee camps: 1998–2003**

Rape Murder Armed robbery Total

Data collected during research in Dadaab, March 2004.

Finally, the funding crisis that has characterised the Kenyan refugee programme in recent years has provoked security concerns. The budget for food assistance in the Dadaab camps, which house the vast majority of Kenya's Somali refugees, was successively reduced by 20% annually in 1999, 2000 and 2001. As a result, there have been several critical interruptions in the food supply to Dadaab. Not only do refugees receive insufficient quantities of food, but they also receive insufficiently diverse food, with no meat or fresh vegetables, in addition to lacking essential non-food items. The shortfalls in aid distribution have also been a cause of insecurity in the Dadaab camps, in some cases leading to violence and murder.

Coupled with the physical insecurity experienced by refugees during the 1990s, the rising grievances of the local population and the increase in conflict between the host community and refugees became a significant concern for local authorities and UNHCR. A series of programmes were designed and implemented in the late 1990s, with the primary objective of reducing levels of physical insecurity for refugees, but with the secondary objective of addressing local grievances and the perception of refugees as a local security concern. The most significant programmes to be introduced were: the 'security package', designed to strengthen the Kenyan police's capacity to enforce law and order in and around the refugee camps by providing them with additional equipment, facilities and incentives; the mobile court, designed to enhance access to justice for victims of crime in Dadaab; and thirdly, the fire-wood project, designed to reduce levels of sexual violence against refugee girls and women during firewood collection by directly provid-ing 30% of their firewood needs.[22] The firewood project has done much to mitigate local conflict over scarce resources.

As a result of these interventions, since 1998 there has been a tenfold reduction in the level of violent crime in and around the Dadaab camps, and the firewood project is given primary credit for this change (see Figure 1).

While the results of these interventions are impressive, they are no substitute for a resolution of the conflict in Somalia or a solution to the Somali refugee situation. As Chapter 4 will outline in more detail, there has recently been progress in these areas, with advances in both the election of a Somali parliament and support for a Comprehensive Plan of Action for the Somali refugee situation, not only in Kenya and the sub-region, but also the Somali diaspora in Europe. However, these advances have been tentative at best, and will only lead to a comprehensive solution if they learn from the failures of past interventions in Somalia, both military and humanitarian, and address the full range of security concerns of both the country of origin and host states like Kenya.

Refugees from Burundi in Tanzania

During the past 30 years, Burundi has experienced several violent upheavals in which hundreds of thousands of refugees have fled across Tanzania's borders. Following the seizure of power in 1972 by the Tutsi minority in Burundi, the Micombero regime unleashed a campaign of 'selective genocide' against the Hutu population resulting in an estimated 80,000–200,000 deaths in Burundi, and the flight of some 150,000 refugees, primarily to Tanzania.[23] In a similar series of events, the 1993 campaign of the Tutsi-dominated army to eliminate Hutu influence within the transi-tional government led to the exodus of an additional 500,000 people into neighbouring countries. While many of these refugees returned home in the following months, Burundi remains wracked by ethnic violence and political instability, causing additional refugees to flee. By December 1997, Tanzania was hosting approximately 230,000 refugees from Burundi, many of whom had arrived in the previous months. This figure did not, however, include an estimated 180,000 Burundian refugees who had arrived in the 1970s, and who had been locally integrated and were no longer registered as refugees with UNHCR.

Until the mid-1990s, Tanzania was reputedly one of the most hospita-ble countries of asylum in Africa.[24] Through the 1960s and 1970s, Tanzania hosted tens of thousands of refugees fleeing both wars of national liberation in Southern Africa and post-colonial conflict and repression in neighbouring states, including Rwanda and Burundi.[25] The Tanzanian government provided ample land for refugee settlements, and refugees were encouraged to achieve self-sufficiency, and many entered the local workforce.[26] This reputation changed dramatically with renewed conflict and genocide in Burundi and Rwanda during the 1990s. Tanzania's refugee population tripled from 292,100 at the end of 1992 to 883,300 at the end of 1994.[27] This mass influx of refugees resulted in a number of pressures on refugee-populated areas in Western Tanzania, including increased crime and insecurity, environmental degradation, and disruption to the local economy.[28] In response to these problems, and in the midst of the country's first multi-party presidential elections, Tanzania ended its long-standing 'open-door' asylum policy, and closed its border with Burundi on 31 March 1995 to prevent the arrival of additional refugees.[29] Tanzania then decided to close the camps for Rwandans and expel the refugee population in December 1996.

The expulsion of tens of thousands of Rwandan refugees has not resulted in an alleviation of Tanzania's refugee-related concerns. In fact, since 1997 the government has formulated and implemented a series of increasingly restrictive refugee policies, justified largely on the grounds that the long-term presence of refugees, especially Burundians, poses both direct and indirect security concerns. The direct concerns have included the alleged presence of armed elements in and around the refugee camps and the link between refugees and the flow of small arms into Tanzania. Indirect concerns have included rising crime (especially following reductions in assistance to refugees) and tensions between refugees and the local population.

Starting in 1997, and in response to increasing security problems within the camps and in the refugee-populated areas, coupled with allegations from the Burundian government that rebels were based in and around the refugee camps, 'the Tanzanian government ordered the army to round-up all foreigners living outside the refugee camps, asserting that this was necessary to protect Tanzanian citizens living close to the border with Burundi.'[30] This approach was rooted in reports that Burundian rebel groups were active in Western Tanzania, and that the ensuing threat was therefore best addressed by confining all Burundians to camps.

This increasingly securitised view of refugees motivated the passing of more restrictive refugee legislation in 1998.[31] During the year, Burundian officials alleged that the refugee camps in Tanzania served as rebel military bases, a charged denied by Dar es Salaam.[32] Relations between Burundi and Tanzania became increasingly strained as a result of these allegations.

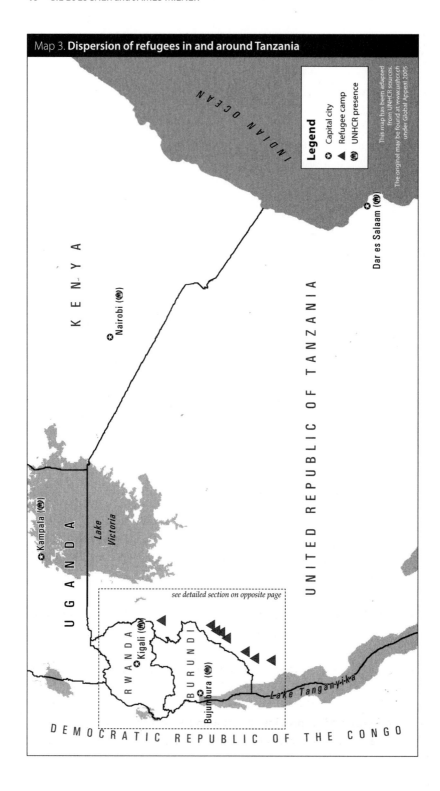

Map 3. **Dispersion of refugees in and around Tanzania**

Legend

⊕ Capital city

◀ Refugee camp

(UN) UNHCR presence

This map has been adapted from UNHCR sources. The original may be found at www.unhcr.ch under Global Appeal 2005.

INDIAN OCEAN

⊕ Dar es Salaam (UN)

KENYA

⊕ Nairobi (UN)

UNITED REPUBLIC OF TANZANIA

⊕ Kampala (UN)

UGANDA

Lake Victoria

see detailed section on opposite page

RWANDA

⊕ Kigali (UN)

BURUNDI

⊕ Bujumbura (UN)

Lake Tanganyika

DEMOCRATIC REPUBLIC OF THE CONGO

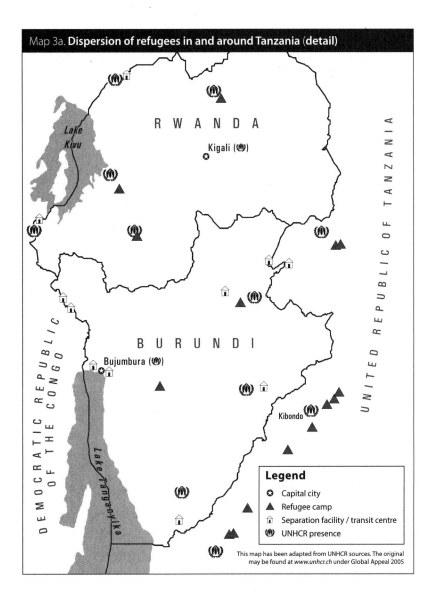

Map 3a. **Dispersion of refugees in and around Tanzania (detail)**

Legend
- ✪ Capital city
- ▲ Refugee camp
- ⌂ Separation facility / transit centre
- ⍟ UNHCR presence

This map has been adapted from UNHCR sources. The original may be found at *www.unhcr.ch* under Global Appeal 2005

For example, in January 2002, it was reported that three Tanzanian villages close to the border had been shelled by the Burundian army.[33]

In light of these concerns, UNHCR identified maintaining the civilian and humanitarian character of the refugee camps as a primary protection problem affecting refugees in Tanzania. Since 1998, UNHCR has received special US funding of approximately $1.4m a year to support a 'security package' designed to provide material and monetary support to almost 300 Tanzanian police officers in the refugee camps in Western Tanzania.

While the package was generally successful in improving law and order within the refugee camps, it had little discernable impact on security in the wider refugee-populated area.[34]

A second direct security concern affecting the refugee-populated area as a whole is the proliferation of small arms and light weapons. In 2003, President Mkapa stated that 'the truth is that the proliferation of small arms is a result of refugees entering our country, a problem which is beyond our capacity to solve'.[35] The proliferation of small arms is certainly a growing concern in Tanzania, and there is a marked tendency to link this problem to the presence of refugees. Notwithstanding the strong evidence *against* linking the presence of refugees to the proliferation of small arms in Western Tanzania, the president's statement has nonetheless reinforced the perception that the refugees are themselves responsible for this problem.[36].

At the same time, relations between the refugee population and local Tanzanians residents were strained partly as a result of local officials blaming refugees for increased crime and environmental degradation, while also claiming that refugees were taking jobs away from local people. Responding to these concerns, one of the objectives of the 1998 Refugees Act was to 'signal disengagement from the Open Door policy of the Nyerere administration, with a view to making Tanzania a less attractive destination for asylum seekers'.[37] At the same time, it has been argued by one Tanzanian scholar that the Act was intended to 'assure the populace that government is determined to address the problem of seemingly endless refugee influxes which are a direct cause of insecurity, environmental degradation, unemployment, moral decadence and electoral tensions'.[38]

While these restrictions were being imposed, funding shortfalls to the UNHCR's Tanzania programme in 1999 and 2000 led refugees increasingly to turn to crime to cope with the shortfall in assistance. The WFP found that 8% of households admitted that they engage in prostitution or theft as a coping mechanism.[39] Throughout 1999, 'local residents in western Tanzania complained that some among the refugees committed … robberies, crop theft, and poaching in national game reserves'.[40] At the same time, 'humanitarian assistance, despite its inadequacy, provided refugees with better nutrition than many local residents enjoyed',[41] which led to further tensions.

In response to these pressures, Tanzania began to press for the repatriation of Burundian refugees. In meetings between UNHCR and the governments of Burundi and Tanzania in early April 2002, it was agreed that repatriation from Tanzania should be increased, notwithstanding UNHCR's reservations about the viability of returning refugees to rebel-held regions of Burundi. During 2003, some 85,000 refugees were repatriated to Burundi.

Given that these returns coincided with sustained crime and insecurity in the refugee-populated areas of Western Tanzania, additional reductions in food rations, and increased restrictions on refugees' freedom of movement and economic activity, a number of organisations, among them Human Rights Watch, Amnesty International, Refugees International and Refugee Council USA, questioned whether the repatriations were truly voluntary and suggested that conditions in the camps had become so unbearable that many refugees felt compelled to go home.[42]

Given the range of security concerns perceived by Tanzania, and the diminishing international support for the refugee assistance programme, it should come as no surprise that repatriation has been identified by the Tanzanian government as the only solution for the Burundian refugee population, and has pushed for an increase in the number of returns. According to a UNHCR report in June 2004, almost 190,000 refugees had returned since the start of the repatriation programme in 2002, some 50,000 in the first six months of 2004 alone.[43]

Simultaneously, there have been drawn-out political negotiations since the late 1990s, based in Arusha, Tanzania, and guided by African elder statesmen such as Julius Nyerere and Nelson Mandela, to resolve the ongoing conflict between Burundi's government and rebel factions. One of the primary objectives of these talks has been to hold national elections in Burundi and establish a government representing the country's diverse political and ethnic interests.

A marked feature of these negotiations has been the common approach of both governments to the question of refugees. Both Tanzania and Burundi see repatriation as the only viable, long-term solution for the protracted refugee population in Western Tanzania. However, repatriation alone will not resolve the problem. While there have been significant repatriations to Burundi in the past three decades, these have been followed by even larger out-flows of refugees. Because Burundi has a history of recurring ethnic violence, the causes of which have not been fundamentally addressed in negotiations, it is unlikely that the continuing return of tens of thousands of refugees to Burundi since 2002 will be sustainable. The rapid return of masses of refugees to densely populated and ethnically divided Burundi may even contribute to increased instability, despite the presence of some 5,000 peacekeepers. The Burundian protracted refugee case underscores the need for a well-integrated political and humanitarian approach, where political, strategic, economic and humanitarian initiatives are complementary and focused on common objectives.

Map 4. **Refugee camps in Guinea and Sierra Leone**

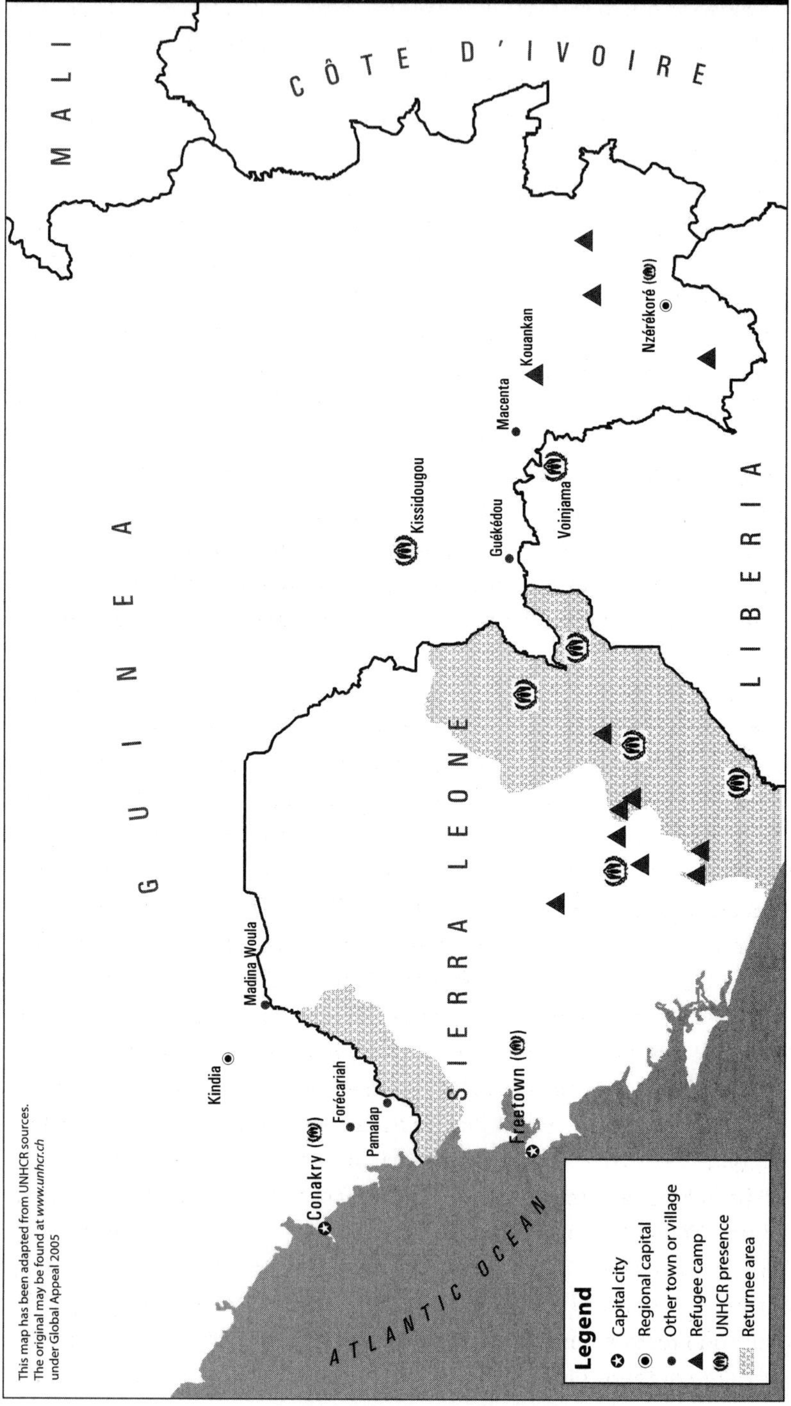
MALI
CÔTE D'IVOIRE
GUINEA
SIERRA LEONE
LIBERIA
ATLANTIC OCEAN
Conakry
Kindia
Forécariah
Pamalap
Madina Woula
Freetown
Kissidougou
Guékédou
Voinjama
Macenta
Kouankan
Nzérékoré
This map has been adapted from UNHCR sources.
The original may be found at www.unhcr.ch
under Global Appeal 2005
Legend
Capital city
Regional capital
Other town or village
Refugee camp
UNHCR presence
Returnee area

Refugees from Liberia and Sierra Leone in Guinea

For most of the 1990s, Guinea was relatively stable while conflict and warlordism engulfed its southern neighbours, Liberia and Sierra Leone.[44] The start of the Liberian civil war in December 1989 resulted in a mass influx of refugees into southern Guinea from January 1990 onwards, reaching 325,000 by the end of the year. From the first arrival of refugees from the Liberian civil war, through the outbreak of the Sierra Leonean conflict in 1991, the 1997 coup d'état in Freetown and the resumption of the Liberian war in 1999, Guinea provided sanctuary for a refugee population that peaked at roughly 670,000 in 1996. At the end of 1999, Guinea hosted an estimated 450,000 refugees: 350,000 from Sierra Leone and 100,000 from Liberia.[45] It was the largest refugee population in Africa.

Throughout the 1990s, the overwhelming majority of refugees in Guinea did not live in refugee camps.[46] Most lived in small-scale refugee settlements, close to the border with Liberia and Sierra Leone. They lived in relative security through most of the decade, pursuing economic self-sufficiency through farming and trade with the local population. This situation began to change in the late 1990s as refugee populations in Guinea became entangled in the emerging sub-regional conflict between factions in Liberia, Sierra Leone and Guinea.

The role that the refugee population and the granting of asylum played in the regional conflict between 1997 and 2003 illustrates how recurring refugee movements, such as the various groups of Liberian refugees arriving in Guinea, can exacerbate regional conflict. Given the security predicament faced by the Guinean regime of Lansana Conté during this period, and its inability to insulate itself from external shocks resulting from the regionalisation of the Liberian conflict, the granting of asylum and the presence of refugees became part of the logic of war. The Guinean state faced a number of security problems relating to the presence of refugees, most notably cross-border attacks on refugee settlements. The effectiveness of various international responses to the conflict in the sub-region and the insecurity in Guinea further highlights the role of protracted refugee situations in regional insecurity, and the need for a resolution of the conflict in the country of origin to achieve true stability in the region as a whole.

The May 1997 coup d'état in Sierra Leone that brought the Armed Forces Revolutionary Council (AFRC) to power, the Economic Community of West African States Monitoring Group (ECOMOG) intervention in February 1998 and the Revolutionary United Front (RUF) attack on Freetown in 1999 all brought successive waves of refugees into not only southern Guinea, but also the capital, Conakry. The fact that

Sierra Leone's ousted president, Ahmed Tejan Kabbah, himself sought refuge in Conakry after the AFRC coup highlighted the importance of asylum in Guinea and its political implications.

These political implications, and the perception that Guinea was using asylum as a means of supporting parties to the conflicts in Sierra Leone and Liberia, became clear after the July 1997 Liberian elections. One of the main opponents of incumbent President Charles Taylor was Alhaji Kromah, a Mandingo, based in southern Guinea and drawing on the support of Liberian refugees in the towns of N'Zérékoré and Macenta. Upon losing the election, Kromah reverted to armed rebellion against Taylor, returning his political party, the All Liberian Coalition Party (ALCOP), to the United Liberation Movement of Liberia for Democracy – K (ULIMO-K), with the open support of Guinea's Lansana Conté.[47]

The response of the Guinean government to the overthrow of Sierra Leonean President Ahmed Tejan Kabbah by the AFRC in 1997 demonstrated the dynamics of allegiances in the sub-region.[48] Two groupings had coalesced in the early 1990s around the mutual distrust between Guinea's Conté and Liberia's Taylor. The first grouping consisted of Presidents Conté and Kabbah, with the support of *Kamajors*, the Sierra Leonean pro-government militia and anti-Taylor ULIMO fighters. The second consisted of Charles Taylor of Liberia, with the support of Sierra Leonean opposition RUF and, to a lesser extent, the AFRC. Refugee protection and assistance became an important aspect of the struggle between these two groupings.[49] The line between refugees and rebels became blurred, as *Kamajors* and ULIMO fighters assisted Guinea's military to patrol its borders and screen those seeking asylum in Guinea and assistance intended for refugees was allegedly diverted to support *Kamajor* and ULIMO campaigns in Sierra Leone and Liberia.

As a result of continued insecurity in both Liberia and Sierra Leone, the refugee population in Guinea continued to grow. By 1999, there were some 300,000 Sierra Leoneans refugees living around the town of Guékédou in southern Guinea, another 50,000 Sierra Leoneans in Forécariah, close to the Guinean capital, Conakry, and approximately 100,000 Liberians living in the forest region of Guinea between Macenta and N'Zérékoré. The non-governmental US Committee for Refugees reported in 2000 that refugee camps in the region were 'dangerously close the border' and that 'following several deadly cross-border raids by Sierra Leonean rebels, Guinea's authorities declared a midnight-to-dawn curfew in some areas'.[50] In response to these attacks, UNHCR moved some 14,000 Sierra Leonean refugees away from the border before the start of the rainy season in July.

As Sierra Leoneans were being relocated, Liberian refugees were being prepared for repatriation. Following the relatively successful Liberian elections of July 1997, UNHCR announced that it would end assistance to Liberians in Guinea at the end of 1999. Some 13,000 Liberians were repatriated in the first eight months of 1999. The repatriation was not, however, sustainable, as over 10,000 Liberians fled to Guinea between April and August as fresh fighting erupted in northern Liberia. This violence again spilled over into Guinea when elements of the Liberian army attacked a Guinean border town near Macenta in September 1999, leaving 27 Guineans dead.[51] As a result, the border was closed and the repatriation suspended.

The intensity and significance of cross-border incursions into Guinea increased significantly in mid-2000. The Liberian civil war escalated, and responding to LURD attacks on Liberia from Guinea in July 2000, Liberian President Charles Taylor initiated a series of incursions by the RUF in conjunction with Liberian armed forces and Guinean dissidents into Guinea. On 2 September 2000, Liberian elements allegedly supported by the RUF attacked the Guinea border town of Massadou, to the east of Macenta. At least 40 Guineans were killed in the attack, which began a rapid chain of violent events. On 4 September, Madina Woula, on the border with Sierra Leone and southeast of the regional centre of Kindia, was attacked, resulting in another 40 deaths. Two days later, on 6 September, Pamalap, the border-town near Forécariah and only 100km from Conakry, was attacked and held by the RUF.

These seemingly coordinated attacks, spanning the length of Guinea's border with Sierra Leone and Liberia, caused panic in Conakry. On 9 September 2000, President Conté addressed the nation on television and radio, saying:

> I am giving orders that we bring together all foreigners ... and that we search and arrest all suspects... They should go home. We know that there are rebels among the refugees. Civilians and soldiers, let's defend our country together.[52]

According to Amnesty International, 'the President's speech is widely seen as a decisive turning point in national policy but also as implicit permission to the military, and the Guinean public, to go on the offensive against refugees in Guinea'.[53] Refugees in Conakry were particularly affected: approximately 6,000 were detained in the days following the speech. Many more were evicted from their homes and subjected to harassment and abuse, physical and sexual, by their neighbours, the police and members of the youth militia, known as the 'Young Volunteers'.

The Guinean government felt its army – lacking motivation, training and equipment – would not be able to repel the invasion without outside support. Support was found in two groups. First, the government reinforced the alliance between Guinean forces and foreign militias based in Guinea. ULIMO fighters were mobilised along with the Guinean army to defend Macenta and Guékédou. Many of these fighters had either previously been refugees in Guinea, were drawn directly from the refugee population or had family members within the refugee camps, especially Kouankan, near Macenta. Secondly, thousands of young Guineans were recruited as 'Young Volunteers' to reinforce border defences.

The Guinean military, supported by the Young Volunteers and ULIMO, waged a six-month campaign against the incursions. This began on 12 September 2000, when the army launched an offensive to retake Pamalap, including an attack on the Farmoréya Refugee Camp near Forécariah. In the months that followed, attacks and counter-attacks on Macenta, Guékédou and throughout southern Guinea resulted in the deaths of some 1,500 Guineans and the internal displacement of between 100,000 and 350,000.

The conflict also had significant implications for the refugee population. Firstly, tens of thousands were themselves displaced. The majority of the more than 90 refugee settlements near Guékédou were destroyed, along with the refugees' livelihood. In the midst of the conflict, refugees were subject to harassment, forced recruitment (as combatants and or porters), physical and sexual abuse, arbitrary detention, and direct attacks by all sides of the conflict.[54] Finally, the killing of the UNHCR Head of Office in Macenta in September 2000 resulted in the evacuation of all UNHCR staff from field offices and the suspension of all UNHCR activities outside Conakry, leaving some 400,000 refugees without assistance for months.

As the violence subsided in early 2001, UNHCR developed a three-pronged strategy to restore stability to the refugee population and provide security. This strategy included a massive exercise to relocate refugees to new camps, the return of many refugees to Sierra Leone, and efforts to resettle the most vulnerable refugees in third countries. As part of this strategy, a new branch of the Guinean police was formed with support from UNHCR to provide security for humanitarian personnel and to promote law and order in the camps. Building on the success of the 'security package' approach developed in Tanzania and Kenya, UNHCR hoped that the equipping and training of security personnel specifically responsible for the camps would ensure greater security there. However, following violent incidents and allegations of abuse of refugees by the new force, new initiatives were undertaken to provide better operational training to ensure effective policing in the camps. Notably, the Canadian government agreed with the UNHCR to deploy two Royal Canadian Mounted Police (RCMP) officers to southern Guinea in a training and coordination role. The deployment lasted 18 months. While gaps in the camp security arrangements remain,[55] this relatively small-scale Canadian deployment raised the standards of camp security to a level unrecognisable from 2001, contributing significantly to refugee protection in Guinea.

It is, however, clear that these interventions into Guinea made only a limited contribution to increased stability in southern Guinea as a whole. While the relocation of the refugee camps in 2001–02, the establishment of camp security arrangements and the Canadian training all addressed Guinea's security concerns, the fall of Liberia's Taylor regime as a result of armed campaigns supported by Guinea, was probably the single greatest factor leading to increased security. In fact, the end to the incursions into southern Guinea coincided with the capture of Voinjama in northern Liberia by Liberians United for Reconciliation and Democracy (LURD), a group formed out of ULIMO in 2000.[56] This attack was the start of a two-year campaign by LURD, with Guinean support, to bring down Taylor's regime. On 11 August 2003, Taylor stepped down, going into exile in Nigeria. The following week, a peace agreement was signed in Accra, ending Liberia's most recent civil war.

While the Taylor regime's fall has resulted in increased stability both in Guinea and in the sub-region, recent events indicate that there is a real potential for a return to conflict, if Liberia's reconstruction is not fully supported by the international donor community. Despite Liberia's Disarmament, Demobilisation, Rehabilitation and Reintegration (DDRR) programme, supported by the UN Development Programme (UNDP), the continued presence of LURD fighters has significantly affected Guinea's security. Moreover, if the DDRR programme is not effectively implemented, the flow of small arms from Liberia could continue to pose security problems. Because of LURD's inactivity, and the loss of a common objective, many LURD fighters have reportedly drifted back across the border to either benefit from humanitarian assistance or engage in criminal activity.[57]

With the changed situation in Liberia, the facilitated repatriation of Liberian refugees began in November 2004. While tens of thousands of refugees are expected to return to Liberia in the coming years, it is essential that past mistakes are not repeated. The history of conflict in the sub-region shows that if solutions are not comprehensive and fully implemented, the cycle of conflict, displacement and the regionalisation of conflict can easily be repeated.

Refugees from Myanmar in Thailand

Thailand has been a major receiving country for refugees from neighbouring countries over the past five decades. More than one million Vietnamese, Lao, Hmong and Khmer refugees sought refuge in Thailand during and after the conflicts in Indochina,[58] by far the largest refugee burden of any Southeast Asian state. The resolution of these refugee problems was ultimately tied up with Cold War rivalries and regional politics. During the 1980s, particularly in Cambodia, external patrons sustained the continuing resistance to Vietnamese rule in Phnom Penh through military aid and political support and a generously financed humanitarian relief programme to various client refugee warrior groups encamped along Thailand's eastern border. Protracted refugee situations developed, lasting decades in some cases. Indeed, it took until 2004 to resettle the last Lao Hmong refugees (who fought for the United States in Laos during the 1950s and 1960s) from camps and settlements in Thailand.

Since 1984, hundreds of thousands of people have fled fighting, arrest and persecution, forced village relocations, crop destruction and forced labour inside Myanmar. More than 120,000 refugees (including Karen, Karenni, Mon and Shan people) are confined in refugee camps that straddle the 2,400 km border. Others, including Myanmar political dissidents, are urban refugees in Bangkok and Chiang Mai while approximately half a million illegal immigrants live in Thai provincial towns and cities. The nearly two-decade long presence of Myanmar refugees has carried significant implications for both Thai domestic security as well as for regional cooperation and stability.

The long-term presence of Myanmar refugees in Thailand is rooted in the weakness of the Myanmar state and the patterns and consequences of conflict in Myanmar.[59] Soon after Burma assumed independence in 1948, the central government was faced with both a long-standing communist insurgency and a protracted low-intensity conflict involving numerous ethnic minorities seeking autonomy for their border homelands. The Myanmar government and military perceived these conflicts as a direct threat to the survival of the state. Military rule was instituted in 1962; the limited federalist structure that had been designed to accommodate the tribal ethnic minorities was dismantled; and the military embarked on an attempt to unify the country under a single territorial sovereignty and a

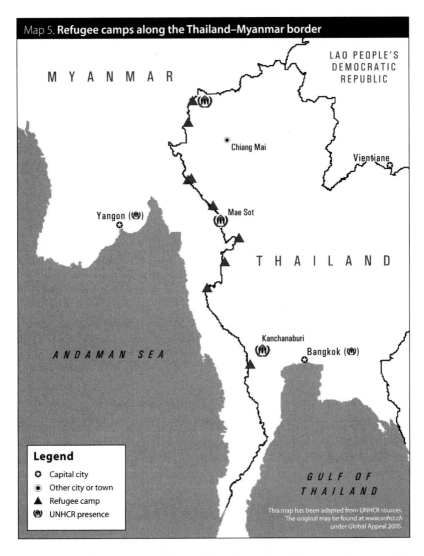

Map 5. **Refugee camps along the Thailand–Myanmar border**

Legend
- ✪ Capital city
- ◉ Other city or town
- ▲ Refugee camp
- (ﬨ) UNHCR presence

This map has been adapted from UNHCR sources. The original may be found at *www.unhcr.ch* under Global Appeal 2005.

strong central government. The military intensified its operations against insurgent strongholds along the border with Thailand, targeting civilians as well as combatants. In 1984 Thailand established camps for Karen and Mon refugees who had fled across the border.[60]

The first major refugee exodus occurred in 1988 when a military junta known as the State Law and Order Restoration Council (SLORC)[61] seized power in Burma after the military's crackdown on widespread political demonstrations. The country was renamed Myanmar. When the National League for Democracy (NLD) led by Aung San Suu Kyi won an overwhelming victory in the 1990 national elections, SLORC declared the election void and began to persecute and murder members of the NLD. Aung San Suu Kyi was placed under house arrest and thousands of her supporters fled to Thailand. Most of these politically active dissidents, called 'students' by Thai authorities, took up residence in Bangkok and other Thai cities. Initially, some of the 'students' were forcibly repatriated to Burma, but by the early 1990s the Thai government recognised that many had a valid fear of persecution. While Thailand is not a signatory to the 1951 Refugee Convention, does not have national refugee status determination procedures, and refused to recognise the 'students' as refugees, it did permit UNHCR to register them and to provide assistance.

During this period, a far greater number of ethnic minority people fled Myanmar army offensives and forced labour and relocation programmes aimed at pacifying and controlling the semi-autonomous border regions. Hundreds of thousands of Karen, Karenni, Mon and Shan poured across the border to Thailand where they have been confined to camps for the past 15 years. Unlike its treatment of the 'students', the Thai government terms the Myanmar ethnic minority groups 'temporarily displaced peoples' and permits UNHCR only limited access to them.

The long-term presence of Myanmar refugees has significant implications for both Thai domestic security as well as for regional cooperation and stability. The refugee problem is a source of inter-state conflict, straining bilateral relations between Thailand and Myanmar and leading to a serious border clash in early 2001. The political activism of Myanmar dissidents in Thailand has long irritated Myanmar's authorities, also damaging bilateral relations. Myanmar 'students' not only held frequent pro-democracy demonstrations in Bangkok and Thai border towns, but they also participated in more extreme forms of activism. For example, on two occasions in 1989 and 1990, Myanmar political dissidents hijacked commercial planes. A group of Karen student activists seized Myanmar's embassy in Bangkok in October 1999 causing a major bilateral crisis and the closure of the border for several months. In January 2000, Karen guerrillas took hundreds of hostages in a Thai provincial hospital raising Thai public and government concerns about the domestic national security threats posed by the presence of Myanmar activists and insurgents on Thai soil.

Throughout recent decades, Thailand and Myanmar have had numerous disputes over the demarcation of their long mountainous border. The 2,400km border is porous and difficult to police, making it easy for refugees, migrant workers and drug smugglers to cross. The long-term presence of refugees on both sides of the border has also been the cause of frequent cross-border military attacks against refugee camps. Beginning in 1995, Myanmar's military and its proxies, such as the Democratic Karen Buddhist Army (DKBN), extended the conflict inside Myanmar to the refugee camps in Thailand. These attacks not only aimed to destroy potential sources of supply and bases for insurgent forces but also a means of obtaining forced labour for their military operations. These incursions violated Thai sovereignty and strained bilateral relations.

The protracted Myanmar refugee situation is also a drain on local resources in an already poor region of Thailand, hindering development efforts and causing local social tensions. [62] Thai communities frequently complain that refugees and illegal migrants compete for local jobs and for natural resources, particularly during periods of economic downturn, such as the late 1990s. Thai labour unions complain that factory owners and businessmen hire illegal workers and refugees because they are cheaper than Thai workers. Consequently, following the economic crisis in 1997, the Thai government came under public pressure, especially from labour unions, to deport large numbers of illegal workers and refugees.

Refugees and migrant workers are frequent scapegoats for social problems in Thailand.[63] Displaced people are viewed as being responsible for health problems along the border and for the increase in trans-border crime. It is estimated that 80% of the sex workers in Thailand are from Myanmar[64] and that women in the border refugee camps, including children as young as 10, are particularly exploited by the sex trade in Thailand. Government authorities have also frequently accused refugees of perpetuating the illegal drug trade, one of Thailand's primary domestic security concerns. Myanmar is the world's second-largest producer after Afghanistan of illicit opium and heroin, and also exports large quantities of amphetamine-type stimulants. These drugs are an important source of income for insurgent movements and diverse criminal activities. Thus, the existence of refugee camps imposes unwelcome demands on the state's central and provincial administrative resources.

In response to these direct and indirect security concerns, the Thai authorities have imposed restriction on refugees from Myanmar in recent years.[65] Some students have been forcibly returned to Myanmar. At the same time, Thailand has recently initiated a policy of relocating all refugees, including 'student' activists, from urban areas to border camps, shutting down UNHCR documentation and assistance programmes for Myanmar 'students' and clamping down on political demonstrations.

Efforts to find a solution to the protracted refugee situation in Thailand have been stymied by the political and military impasse. The military refuses to permit national elections with the NLD or minority-group participation. It continues to use force to quell opposition to its rule and engages in systematic human-rights abuses. Myanmar refugees cannot be repatriated until their physical safety can be assured. Moreover, communities in Myanmar's border regions are among the most impoverished in the world and are not able to support and reintegrate large influxes of returnees without substantial international economic assistance.

Thailand remains opposed to providing any opportunities to integrate Myanmar refugees locally.[66] The government and public increasingly view the Myanmar as a security burden, as a strain on state capacity and as a threat to social cohesion. They resent the actions of Myanmar activists; they see refugees and illegal migrants as competitors for jobs, resources and limited social services; and they perceive Myanmar to be the cause of increased crime and health risks.

There have been regional and bilateral efforts to resolve the political impasse in Myanmar and the refugee problem in Thailand. At the Bagan Summit in November 2003, ASEAN governments initiated an 'economic cooperation strategy' to generate economic development in border regions, particularly between Myanmar and Thailand as a means of creating an 'enabling environment' for solving the refugee problem and for improving bilateral relations. Thailand and Myanmar started 'the Bangkok Process' in December 2003 to encourage democratic reform in Myanmar. Despite these initiatives, very little has changed either regarding the political stalemate in Myanmar or the protracted refugee problem in Thailand.

The overthrow of former Myanmar Prime Minister Khin Nyunt in October 2004 by hardline elements within the military brought political dialogue regarding democratic change in Myanmar to a standstill. Recent bilateral efforts on the part of ASEAN member states to persuade Yangon through a policy of 'constructive engagement' to reform itself have failed, and the UN envoy to Myanmar, Razali Ismail, was refused entry to the country in 2004.

Unlike the international response to the past Indochinese refugee situation, there has been very little external interest or active political engagement in the protracted Myanmar refugee population. Myanmar's energy resources and strategic position means it has powerful economic and diplomatic support from China and India. Pro-business interests in other Southeast and East Asian countries also effectively protect the military junta led by General Tan Shwe from external pressure. In the late 1980s, in response to what was perceived to be a strategically important refugee problem, the United States and other Western governments, regional governments, including Vietnam, and international agencies, adopted a comprehensive region-wide plan of action to deal with the long-term Vietnamese refugee problem. By 1996, durable solutions were found for the great majority of refugees and outward flows of refugees and migrants from Vietnam stopped altogether. Despite recent Western sanctions and threats to boycott meetings held in Yangon, the protracted Myanmar refugee problem does not carry the same geopolitical importance for the West and ASEAN that the Indochinese refugee population did. Vietnam, unlike Myanmar, had strong political and economic motives for cooperating with the US and regional actors. Without a concerted regional effort and sustained international pressure as well as the willingness of Yangon to begin implementing democratic reforms in Myanmar and for all key actors to support regional and international resettlement, repatriation and reintegration of Myanmar refugees, there will be no resolution for the over 120,000 refugees encamped along the Thai–Myanmar border.

The Bhutanese Lhotshampas in Nepal

Approximately 100,000 Bhutanese Lhotshampas have been confined to several refugee camps in southeastern Nepal since the early 1990s. This protracted refugee situation is a source of regional tensions between Nepal, Bhutan and India, and in recent years, Maoist guerrillas have used the camps as recruiting grounds for their insurgency in neighbouring Nepal and the Indian state of Sikkim. The Bhutanese refugee crisis is also the result of ethnic cleansing and, if left unresolved, may set a dangerous precedent for a region rife with ethnic and communal tensions.[67]

The Lhotshampas are descendents of Nepalese immigrants who began immigrate into the southern lowlands of Bhutan during the nineteenth century. Before the 1980s, the Hindu Lhotshampas remained largely unintegrated but were given access to government employment and the opportunity to have Bhutanese citizenship under the Nationality Law of 1958.[68] By the 1980s, however, Bhutan's king and the ruling Buddhist Druk majority expressed concern over the rapidly growing Lhotshampa population. The 1988 census revealed that Bhutan's population was 48% Buddhist, 45% Nepali and 7% 'other'. Concerned over the influx of Nepali migrants into Bhutan and the higher birth rate of the Lhotshampas, the Bhutanese Druks feared that this demographic shift threatened their privileged position and traditional Buddhist culture.

During the 1980s, the Bhutanese authorities adopted a series of ethno-nationalist policies to counter what the monarchy and Druk elites perceived as a potential national security threat. In 1985, the government established new eligibility requirements for Bhutanese citizenship that effectively disen-

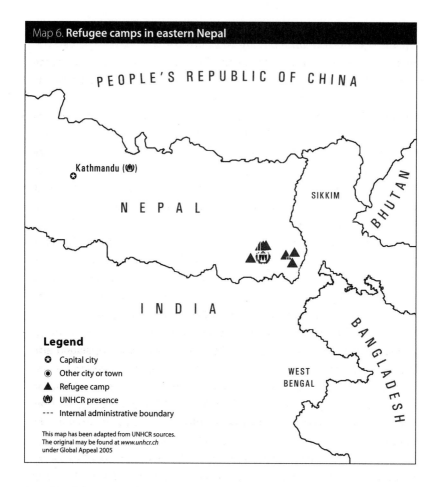

Map 6. **Refugee camps in eastern Nepal**

PEOPLE'S REPUBLIC OF CHINA

Kathmandu (⊕)

SIKKIM

BHUTAN

N E P A L

I N D I A

Legend

⊗ Capital city
◉ Other city or town
▲ Refugee camp
(⊕) UNHCR presence
- - - Internal administrative boundary

This map has been adapted from UNHCR sources.
The original may be found at *www.unhcr.ch*
under Global Appeal 2005

WEST
BENGAL

BANGLADESH

franchised large numbers of ethnic Nepalis, depriving them of both their citizenship and civil rights. In addition, the government introduced measures to enforce rigidly the Druka dress code, forbid the use of Nepali language in the national educational curriculum, and require special permission for entrance to schools and to sell cash crops. Throughout this period, Bhutan's king, Jigme Singye, rationalised these nationalist restrictions by telling visiting journalists, diplomats and scholars 'that Bhutan was a small nation between giant neighbours, that all it had to define itself was its cultural identity, and that it was too small to enjoy the luxury of cultural pluralism'.[69]

These drastic measures occurred during a period of heightened security concerns on the part of the monarchy and Druk elite. As a small state in the Himalayas wedged between two powerful neighbours, Bhutan is acutely sensitive to shifts in regional politics. During recent decades, the government has felt increasingly vulnerable as a result of alarming political and security developments in the region. Since the 1950s, and particularly after the Chinese annexation of Tibet, Bhutan became very dependent on India for trade and economic relations. With a change in the Himalayan balance of power, the Bhutanese authorities increasingly became fearful of Indian hegemony. In 1974, India annexed the ethnic Nepali-dominated state of Sikkim, raising further concerns that a similar outcome awaited neighbouring Bhutan if the Nepali-speaking Lhoshampas' influence grew. In the mid-1980s, militant separatist movements advocating independence for the ethnic-Nepali dominated Indian northeastern states of Assam and Darjeeling and operating out of southern Bhutan increased the Druk majority's sense of vulnerability to the possibility of violent Indian reaction. Finally, events in neighbouring Nepal greatly unsettled Bhutan's court. In 1990, Nepal replaced its absolute monarchy with a constitutional monarchy; subsequent Nepali popular calls for democratisation and self-determination and the rapid rise of violent opposition to the monarchy in the form of a Maoist-led insurgency intensified Bhutan's fears over the potential for political activism on the part of the Lhoshampas.

When the Lhoshampa minority in southern Bhutan began to organise politically in the late 1980s to lobby against restrictive legislation and measures that violated their human rights, the authorities declared these activities seditious and unlawful. Some Lhoshampas became activists in the Bhutanese People's Party, which called for Bhutan's democratisation. Large-scale protests broke out in 1990, resulting in violent clashes with the police and army and mass arrests. The authorities increased their intimidation of the Lhoshampas in southern Bhutan by destroying their property, arbitrarily detaining and torturing activists, and forcing individuals to sign so-called 'voluntary migration certificates' before expelling them from the country.[70] In December 1990 Bhutanese authorities announced that residents of Bhutan who could not prove that they immigrated before 1958 must leave. Consequently, tens of thousands of Bhutanese Lhoshampas were made stateless and in 1990–92 fled to Nepal and to West Bengal in India.

Since the early 1990s, over 100,000 Lhotshampas have been confined to six UNHCR-run refugee camps in southeastern Nepal.[71] Donor governments have spent approximately $20m per year on assistance and protection programmes. In 1998, the quality of basic services was better than in most Nepali villages. Children were provided with education to secondary school level and the Lhotshampa leadership took an active part in administering the camps. However, despite the relatively high standard of the camps, there was considerable frustration among the refugees over their prolonged exile. These frustrations were particularly pronounced among young people, who constituted the highest proportion of the refugee population and for whom there were few opportunities for further education and employment. As protracted exile has continued, since the late 1990s, suicide rates have increased as have domestic violence, alcoholism, sexual exploitation by international and Nepali government officials, and trafficking of women and children.[72]

There is only limited local integration of the refugees with the local population. The Lhotshampa have provided cheap labour, particularly in the construction industry, increased the numbers of goods and stalls in local markets, and have improved services to the local populace who have been allowed access to health care in the camps. At the same time, though, Nepali villagers complain that the refugees compete for local employment and drive down wages, depress prices in the markets by selling their UNHCR rations, and contribute to rising local crime and prostitution.

Nepal's overriding principal domestic security concern, however, is the threat posed by the growing Maoist guerrilla insurgency. This focus on internal security has been exacerbated in the last two years following the disbanding of the Nepalese parliament and the imposition of a state of emergency by the Nepalese monarchy.[73] The government in Kathmandu is concerned about a possible nexus between Maoist groups, the Lhotshampa refugees and the United Liberation Front of Assam which has bases in southern Bhutan. Nepali Maoists already carry our active propaganda and recruiting activities in the refugee camps in southeastern Nepal. The authorities fear that as frustrations with protracted exile accumulate, particularly among refugee youths, the camps may pose a direct security threat to the government.

By 2005, a solution to the protracted refugee situation in Nepal remained as elusive as ever. Since 1993, there have been more than a dozen interministerial meetings between the governments of Bhutan and Nepal to try to resolve the Lhotshampa refugee crisis. In December 2001, the Joint Ministerial Committee finally agreed on a joint refugee nationality verification process and began work verifying the nationalities of the residents of one camp. However, the process has been plagued with problems and has been severely criticised by international observers for failing to meet international standards.[74] The process excluded UNHCR and involved only representatives from the governments of Bhutan and Nepal. Under the verification scheme, more than 70% of camp residents were classified as 'voluntary migrants' on the grounds that they signed 'voluntary migration forms' when leaving Bhutan. Yet most refugees were required to sign such forms under duress before being permitted to leave. In some cases, members of the same family were placed in different categories so they risk separation in the event of eventual repatriation. Some refugees who were minors in Bhutan and who did not possess identity documents before they fled were classified as non-Bhutanese even though their parents possessed identity papers. It appears that the identification and verification process was intended to render stateless large numbers of Nepali-speaking Bhutanese.

In the face of almost total refusal by Bhutanese authorities to lift their ethno-nationalist restrictions and permit the repatriation of the Lhotshampa refugees, UNHCR, with the backing of major Western donor governments, announced in 2003 its intention to encourage and promote local integration in Nepal as the preferred solution. As of mid-2005, however, it was unclear how effective this policy would be. The government of Nepal opposed local integration of the refugees, preferring to work towards their eventual repatriation to Bhutan. The plan is also opposed by the majority of refugee leaders in Nepal, who also view repatriation as the only durable solution. International observers, particularly human-rights organisations, consider Bhutanese behaviour towards the Lhotshampas to constitute ethnic cleansing and believe that to sanction such state actions would set a dangerous precedent for the region and might result in further expulsions of minorities not only from Bhutan but also from other neighbouring South Asian countries. [75]

* * *

These five cases illustrate that the presence of long-staying refugee populations exacerbates the internal and external vulnerabilities of weak host states and is perceived by the central governments and local populations of these countries as factors that not only pose threats to national security and sovereignty but also threaten domestic stability and weaken local governance and local economies. Understanding the nature of direct and indirect security concerns that protracted refugee situations pose to many host governments and societies in Africa and Asia is a prerequisite to establishing appropriate policy responses. Those responses necessarily have to be broad-based and integrated in order to deal with the complex security, development and humanitarian problems created by protracted refugee situations today. The following chapter aims to inform the policy debates on protracted refugee situations by developing a comprehensive framework for resolving or mitigating at least some of these problems in the future.

CHAPTER FOUR

Towards solutions for protracted refugee situations

Because the causes and consequences of the security concerns provoked by protracted refugee populations are diverse, it is impossible to formulate a single policy response to all migration-related security concerns. In fact, the elements of a necessary response are varied and different programmes are required at different stages of a response. This chapter considers efforts to address various aspects of protracted refugee situations before proposing a framework for the planning and implementation of comprehensive plans of action for individual protracted refugee situations.

In the short term, it is important for the international humanitarian and donor community to address the security implications of protracted refugee situations. Direct security concerns should be tackled by supporting the separation and exclusion of armed elements within the refugee population, despite the highly complex nature of this undertaking.[1] Specific disarmament measures, such as UN arms embargos, have to be enforced. Disarmament programmes must be fully implemented; militias and warlords must be demobilised and, in some cases, integrated into the national army and police; and arms syndicates and networks need to be broken.

In recent years, UNHCR has developed a range of operational responses to deal with the problem of militarisation of refugee camps. In 1999, it introduced a 'ladder of options' to prepare and respond to these situations. Three options were proposed under this initiative: 'soft options', including preventive measures and cooperation with national law-enforcement authorities; 'medium options', including the deployment of civilian or police monitors; and 'hard options', including military deployment.[2] Following this policy direction, UNHCR introduced Humanitarian Security Officer and military advisers from the Department of Peacekeeping Operations (DPKO) and the Canadian government in selected African camps. UNHCR's first efforts to implement its new policy response to armed elements in refugee camps involved implementing the 'security package' in western Tanzania and northern Kenya, and the relocation exercise in Guinea. While these actions helped create greater security for some refugee camps and communities, they have not uniformly led to greater security in the wider refugee-populated areas.[3] A similar effort by UNHCR and the DPKO in the Democratic Republic of the Congo in mid-2001 successfully separated armed elements from refugees.[4]

From these experiences, it is evident that the future success of the 'ladder of options' depends on the practical partnerships and 'security packages' that UNHCR is able to form with the DPKO and governments and regional organisations. While discussions between DPKO and UNHCR have laid the groundwork for future cooperation between the two offices, serious differences of approach and political and resource constraints remain. On the one hand, UNHCR and other humanitarian aid organisations fear that too close an association with the military compromises their impartiality and neutrality, and on the other, governments are reluctant to authorise the use of military forces for such functions. Protection for refugees in conflict zones and unstable border regions also depends critically on the willingness and ability of host states and countries of origin to observe international humanitarian norms regarding the treatment of refugees and non-combatants.

In the last two years there has been a dramatic increase in the number of UN peacekeeping operations in Africa. The UN Security Council has authorised new missions in Liberia and Burundi and has strengthened existing ones in the Democratic Republic of the Congo. It has authorised a large-scale mission to southern Sudan to support the implementation of a comprehensive peace accord signed at the end of 2004. These missions are overwhelmingly staffed by troops from developing countries and many commentators feel the UN is dangerously over-stretched in its peacekeeping operations.

Such African missions are also so-called complex peacekeeping operations, involving multiple tasks and combining military and civilian components.[5] Building up regional peacekeeping capabilities goes hand in hand with development initiatives to help restore stability in war torn regions. But as Berdal points out, neither the DPKO nor the under-resourced peacekeeping forces from developing countries have adequate capacity (especially in logistics) to sustain this level of multiple operations effectively.[6] A crucial problem is the enormous amount of time it takes to mobilise and deploy peacekeeping forces into regions of conflict. Therefore, there is an urgent need to address how governments and the UN should respond to the problems of incapacity in African peacekeeping and how to empower regional bodies to assist in meeting this challenge.

The November 2004 commitment by European Union defence ministers to create thirteen 1,500-strong battle groups, deployable within 10 days of political action, is an effort to fill this gap. It is expected that the battle groups' main area of operations will be Africa. They will be mandated to intervene by the UN Security Council or at the request of a government and would be expected to enforce a ceasefire and deal with a civil emergency until a UN or African Union peacekeeping force could be mobilised and deployed. The UK and Canada have also offered to train African Union forces for deployment as peacekeepers and stabilisation forces in several African conflicts.

As with responding to the direct security concerns, responding to indirect threats requires the engagement of diverse actors and agencies. Unlike direct threats, however, indirect threats are best addressed in the short to medium term through development initiatives and targeted assistance designed to address burdens imposed on local communities by hosting of refugees, and to ease tensions between refugees and the local community. Most often, these interventions can be small scale and highly focused. In the long term, however, the security implications of protracted refugee situations are best addressed through comprehensive solutions, involving a broad range of policy interventions.

Northern Kenya provides an example of how small-scale and highly focused development initiatives can help address the security implications of refugee movements by improving the security of not only refugee-populated areas, but also the security of the host state as a whole. In response to alarming levels of insecurity in and around the Dadaab refugee camps, in the late 1990s, UNHCR intervened various ways in Kenya, including the firewood project.

The six years following the introduction of the firewood project in 1998 witnessed a dramatic decline not only in the number of reported cases of rapes in the three Dadaab camps, but also in murder and armed robbery. UN and NGO workers in Dadaab believe that this improvement in refugee security and the dramatic decline in violent crime has been overwhelmingly the result of the firewood project and its positive secondary benefits of creating jobs for the local population while encouraging young men who would otherwise pursue banditry to participate in the more lucrative firewood trade.

The firewood project thereby mitigates the indirect security burden in Kenya in several ways. Firstly, it reduces the strain on a scarce environmental resource in and around Dadaab by ensuring that firewood is collected in a managed way across a wider area. Secondly, it ensures an income to the local population, thereby reducing grievances that may arise between refugees and Kenya. Thirdly, by providing a context within which the refugees and the local population can cooperate in a large-scale, mutually beneficial project, better understanding is developed between the two groups, which serves as an important basis for future local conflict resolution.

The presence of refugees and refugee programmes, could, if effectively managed, significantly contribute to longer-term local and national development.[7] In the case of Kenya, the benefits of the refugee presence has been experienced at the national level, especially through the large amount of foreign currency brought into Kenya as a result of humanitarian activities, and at the local level, through contributions to the local economy, job creation and improvements to local infrastructure. In addition to these benefits, the local community has also been supported through the Local Assistance Project (LAP), managed primarily by CARE Kenya, UNHCR's implementing partner in Dadaab.[8] This programme grew out of a realisation in the mid-1990s that the gap in livelihoods between refugees and the local population was large, growing and a significant source of conflict between the two groups. Since their initiation, LAPs have made significant contributions to the local community through schools, water, agro-forestry and training, totalling some $13m over the past 10 years. In addition, UNHCR contributes over $1m a year to the local police, has invested more than Ksh35m (approximately $446,000) since 1995 in the rehabilitation and improvement of roads and airstrips in the Dadaab region, and has constructed and maintained almost 30 water boreholes for the local population since 1992.

Unresolved protracted refugee situations perpetuate poverty and social and political deprivation. The World Bank notes three dimensions of poverty: lack of income and assets; voicelessness and powerlessness in the institutions of state and society; and inability to cope with shocks, such as sudden changes in currency values or market forces. The UNHCR argues that refugees suffer from all three conditions and that poverty can also lead refugees to resort to coping mechanisms that may be illegal and sources of local tension, such as theft, prostitution and banditry.[9] Development programmes can play a key role in addressing some of these indirect security burdens by providing safety nets for refugees. There is, therefore, a double benefit in the short to medium term: development-related projects targeting refugee populated areas can foster greater security and protection for refugees and the local population, while also contributing to broader national development objectives.

Towards a full response: comprehensive solutions to protracted refugee situations

Such directed interventions do not, however, provide a full response to the security implications of refugee movements or chronic refugee problems. These interventions can only help manage the situation until a resolution can be found. In the long term, the security implications of forced migration can only be fully addressed by formulating and implementing comprehensive solutions for protracted refugee scenarios. Such a response would employ the full range of possible solutions for refugees – repatriation and reintegration, local integration in the host country, and resettlement in a third country.

Comprehensive solutions to long-term refugee populations based on the three durable solutions are not new. Such an approach was central to resolving the situation of displaced people in Europe long after the Second World War, and of millions of Indochinese and Central American refugees in the 1980s and 1990s. By approaching the particular character of each refugee situation, and by considering the needs, concerns and capacities of the countries of first asylum, the country of origin, resettlement and donor countries, along with the needs of refugees themselves, the international donor community has successfully resolved the plight of numerous refugee populations in the past 50 years. Similar creativity, compassion and commitment are needed now to resolve similar refugee problems, and to address the growing concerns of Western asylum countries, countries in the regions of refugee origin and the increasingly dire lack of protection for millions of refugees.

Towards the end of the 1950s, concerned individuals in Europe drew attention to the plight of the residual caseload of tens of thousands of people displaced in Europe after 1945 who were still in need of a solution. British refugee advocates, backed by NGOs and UNHCR, called for international action by governments.[10] This pressure resulted in 1959 being declared 'World Refugee Year' by the United Nations, and the initiation of a comprehensive response to those remaining both in and outside camps. Following UNHCR's appeal to major Western governments to provide both funds and resettlement quotas, this protracted refugee problem was finally resolved by the mid-1960s. This response to 'the residual groups left behind after successive selection missions have picked those people who were young and healthy and met rigid resettlement criteria',[11] motivated by humanitarian concern, illustrates the potential for a comprehensive reset-tlement effort to address the needs of protracted and neglected refugee caseloads. This programme is an often-forgotten precedent for addressing the durable solution and protection needs of refugees for whom neither local integration nor repatriation are viable options.

The international response to the Indochinese refugee crisis in Southeast Asia during the 1980s is a second important example of a comprehensive solution. In response to public outcry at the dire conditions of thousands of 'boat people' who had fled Vietnam, and those who had left Cambodia and Laos overland, and following dramatic steps by other southeast Asian countries to prevent the arrival of the asylum-seekers, concerned states gathered at an International Conference on Indo-Chinese Refugees in July 1979.[12] Western states agreed to increase dramatically the number of refu-gees they resettled from the region. In exchange, it was agreed that the boat people would be recognised as refugees *prima facie*, that illegal departures would be prevented and that regional processing centres would be estab-lished. The result was a formalised *quid pro quo*: resettlement in Western states in exchange for assurances of first asylum in the region.

While immediate results were positive, the number of asylum-seekers began to rise sharply in 1988 as promises of resettlement resulted in a dramatic pull factor. It was clear that the new arrivals constituted a mixed flow of refugees and economic migrants, and that a satisfactory solu-tion could not be achieved without the cooperation of a wide range of actors. A Second International Conference on Indo-Chinese refugees was convened in June 1989 and concluded by adopting the Comprehensive Plan of Action for Indochinese Refugees (CPA). The CPA comprised five mechanisms by which the countries of origin, countries of first asylum and resettlement countries cooperated to resolve the refugee crisis in Southeast Asia: an Orderly Departure Program (ODP) to prevent clandestine depar-tures, guaranteed temporary asylum by countries in the region, individual refugee status determination for all new arrivals, resettlement to third coun-tries for those recognized as refugees, and facilitated return for rejected claimants.[13] Notwithstanding a number of criticisms,[14] the CPA is seen to have generally achieved its objectives of reducing the number of clandes-tine departures, managing the flow of migrants from Southeast Asia and of finding extra-regional durable solutions for recognised refugees.

In contrast to the CPA, where resettlement was identified as the primary durable solution, the International Conference on Central American Refugees (CIREFCA), also convened in 1989, placed the greatest emphasis on return and reintegration, supported by selected projects on local integration, as the primary durable solution.[15] Following a series of peace agreements ending over a decade of conflict of civil war in El Salvador, Nicaragua and Guatemala, CIREFCA was an integral part of the wider objective of consolidating peace in the region. Through a series of development initiatives for returning refugees, capacity-building initiatives targeting states and NGOs, and the integration of refugees and returnees into national and regional development strategies, CIREFCA formulated a comprehensive solution appropriate to the needs and priorities in the region.

These three examples demonstrate how comprehensive solutions may effectively respond to the challenges of protracted refugee situations. While each approach used different combinations of the three durable solutions, they all represent concerted efforts by a wide range of actors to address the particular needs of individual refugee problems. As recently noted by members of the UNHCR's Executive Committee at the conclusion of a two-year long series of consultations with UNHCR on the future of international refugee policy there is a need for 'more coherence in integrating voluntary repatriation, local integration, and resettlement, whenever feasible, into one comprehensive approach, implemented in close cooperation among countries of origin, host States, UNHCR and its humanitarian and development partners, especially NGOs, as well as refugees'.[16]

Enhancing the three durable solutions

The formulation of comprehensive solutions to protracted refugee situations must be preceded by sustained efforts by UNHCR, donor governments and host countries to build on recent developments to reinforce the three durable solutions. Firstly, there is a need to improve local integration prospects and prospects for durable solutions within the region of refugee origin. Referred to by some as the 'forgotten solution',[17] comparatively little attention was paid by UNHCR to enhancing local integration prospects throughout the 1990s when both UNHCR and donor states were focused on emergency responses to large refugee emergencies. As a consequence, host states in the regions of refugee origin are now opposed to local integration, viewing the presence of refugees on their territory as temporary, and maintaining that every refugee entering their territory will either repatriate to their country of origin or will be resettled to a third country.

A number of host and donor governments, in addition to UNHCR, have, however, recently recognised that refugees cannot be held indefinitely in camps, and that 'the promotion of self-reliance of refugees is an important means to avoid dependency, take advantage of the initiative and potential contributions of refugees, and prepare them for durable solutions'.[18]

In this way, UNHCR has increasingly focused on improving prospects for durable solutions through development aid directed to refugee-populated areas. This targeting of development assistance to countries hosting large refugee populations over protracted periods was a priority for former High Commissioner for Refugees, Ruud Lubbers. In particular, he promoted two possible approaches: Development Assistance for Refugees (DAR) and Development through Local Integration (DLI). These initiatives were important steps towards implementing a more holistic approach by developing linkages between refugee issues and national and regional development agendas. While lessons need to be drawn from past efforts to merge refugee and development issues, especially in Africa,[19] donor states, individually and collectively, should recognise the benefits of such an approach.

Donor governments could support local integration by encouraging host states to consider making refugees more self-reliant by targeting assistance to refugee-populated areas and by supporting self-sufficiency initiatives for locally integrated refugees. Donor governments should also understand how policy initiatives such as externally imposed democratisation and economic liberalisation have contributed to increased reluctance by many African states to integrate refugees locally. Sustained donor commitment to refugee integration programmes and to understanding the political and economic constraints on many host states would undoubtedly encourage hosts to be more generous and innovative. Unfortunately, at present, although seven out of ten refugees are located in developing countries, assistance for them is inadequate and only provided erratically. Providing consistent, adequate levels of assistance would be the first step to convincing over-burdened host countries to offer permanent legal status as a complement to self-sufficiency.

Secondly, there have been significant developments since the late 1990s in resettlement policy and practice. Resettlement has increasingly been recognised as a valuable means of protection for individual refugees, as a potential durable solution for groups of refugees, and as a tangible expression of international solidarity with countries of first asylum. To this end, there has been some consideration of how resettlement, used strategically, may enhance the protection environment and local integration prospects of those refugees left in camps.[20] Resettlement is also increasingly seen as an important component of any comprehensive solution for protracted refugee scenarios.[21]

There are, however, significant constraints on global resettlement efforts.[22] The overwhelming majority of long-term refugees could be eligible for resettlement, but a lack of resettlement opportunities, of resettlement staff to prepare submissions, and inefficiencies in the process of preparing and submitting resettlement cases have resulted in the under-utilisation of this durable solution. In light of the role that resettlement has played in past comprehensive solutions, notably the Indochinese CPA, it is clear that these constraints must be addressed in order to find comprehensive solutions. To this end, the development of a Europe-wide resettlement programme, including a significant expansion of resettlement opportunities there, could play a significant role in future comprehensive solutions.[23]

Thirdly, the solution that is probably most appropriate for the majority of refugees, and certainly the solution that is preferred by many states, is repatriation. During the 1990s, states and UNHCR moved away from voluntary repatriation to the notion of return in 'conditions of safety and dignity'.[24] However, repatriation to Angola, Burundi and Liberia, for example, has demonstrated that premature repatriation followed by further displacement and return to exile can be more traumatic for refugees and costly for the refugee protection regime than delaying the repatriation until the political, security and economic conditions in the country of origin have improved sufficiently to support large-scale return and reintegration.

Repatriation is not simply the process of returning home. There is a need to ensure that homecoming is durable: that the preconditions for effective and secure repatriation, including a monitored peace agreement and international commitment to ensuring its sustainability, are in place. As frustrations with the repatriation of Afghan refugees from Pakistan and Iran in recent years have clearly illustrated, refugees are reluctant to return to their country of origin if there is continued insecurity and an apparent decline in international support. In this light, UNHCR has encouraged states to invest in more sustainable return and reintegration programmes, revolving around the '4 Rs': repatriation, reintegration, rehabilitation and reconstruction.

Following discussions on comprehensive solutions for the most prominent protracted refugee situations,[25] in March 2004 UNHCR hosted a series of meetings to generate international support for the repatriation of several refugee populations in Africa. UNHCR argued that conditions in countries like Somalia, Liberia, Burundi, Sudan, Sierra Leone and Angola were suitable for the preparation of large-scale returns in the coming years, pending progress in the relevant peace processes and in the ability of UNHCR and partner agencies to build the capacity in host countries to receive and reintegrate the returning populations. In one example, UNHCR subsequently appealed to the international donor community for $39.2m to support the return and reintegration of both refugees and internally displaced persons in Liberia, but received only $3m. While repatriation is not immediately possible, sufficient investment will be essential to ensure that the infra-structure is in place to support repatriation.

Return and reintegration programmes are an example of the dramatic action needed to correct the highly selective nature of most donor funding for protracted refugee problems. Hitherto, funding for humanitarian programmes has largely reflected the foreign and domestic policies of donor governments.[26] Such behaviour does not provide a coherent or effective system for financing international humanitarian activities. Donor governments give vastly disproportionate amounts of aid to a few well-known cases and far lesser aid to dozens of less well-publicised refugee problems. The absence of an autonomous resource base for UNHCR, similar to government-assessed contributions to other UN operations, for example, continues to limit the response to present and future refugee crises. While the UNHCR has recently tried to overcome these financial constraints by trying to access funding from national development agencies, such as the UK Department for International Development (DfID), and international development organisations, such as UNDP, to finance unmet needs, it is not clear that this will work. Donor governments need to work towards a strengthened multilateral regime with the mandate, capacity and resources to meet current unmet refugee needs in a more impartial and effective manner.

Recent interest in responses to protracted refugee situations

These moves towards individual durable solutions have not been matched by a more comprehensive effort to deal with long-standing refugee popu-lations. A few key studies by practitioners addressed this issue in the 1970s and 1980s.[27] More recently, the Evaluation and Policy Analysis Unit at UNHCR undertook a series of studies on the issue.[28] While these studies provide important insights into cases in Africa and elsewhere, the primary focus has been on addressing refugees' daily security concerns and not on the wider security ramifications.

During the current decade, however, the rising importance of long-term refugee problems has been given a higher profile within intergovernmental settings. In December 2001, there was an African Ministerial Meeting on protracted refugee situations[29] and the issue has been considered at recent UNHCR Executive Committee sessions[30] as well as within the framework of the UNHCR Global Consultations on Refugee Protection.[31] While there was some preliminary discussion on comprehensive solutions for the most prominent long-term refugee problems,[32] discussions focused largely on issues of livelihood and burden-sharing and not on either the links between regional security and chronic refugee situations or on the security problems refugees pose for host countries in regions of refugee origin.

Policy discussions in recent years have also tended to concentrate on the need to develop refugees' potential to engage in economically productive activities, to foster refugees as 'agents of development', and promote community-based assistance, including aid to host communities, as a pillar of UNHCR's future programmes. While recent research has highlighted how the long-term presence of refugees can promote infrastructural development and state-building,[33] there appears to be little recognition of the history of UNHCR's earlier and often unsuccessful efforts to promote self-reliance in Africa's rural refugee settlements.[34] The current policy proposals and solutions advanced by UNHCR and others need to be examined critically within a historical perspective so as not simply to repeat past policy failures.[35]

Since 2004, UNHCR's thinking has started to consider a broader range of political aspects of both the causes of protracted refugee scenarios and their preconditions. In a June 2004 paper, UNHCR recognised that 'as the causes of persistent refugee situations are political, solutions must be sought in that arena' and that it was important for the organization to 'understand the political forces and opportunities' underpinning responses to chronic refugee populations.[36] In September 2004, UNHCR began developing a framework for resolving long-standing refugee situations[37] that recognises not only the differences between historical and contemporary long-standing refugee scenarios, but also the diversity of contemporary cases.

While UNHCR has highlighted the important political dimensions of protracted refugee situations, it has not recognised that it cannot address these dimensions on its own. In fact, UNHCR's specifically non-political mandate precludes it from engaging directly with these political forces independently. While it is essential that agencies involved in protecting refugees are sensitive to host governments' security concerns regarding chronic refugee populations, actions by humanitarian agencies, such as UNHCR, without the support of peace and security actors, such as the UN Security Council, will not lead to truly comprehensive solutions. So long as discussions on protracted refugee situations remain exclusively within the humanitarian community, and do not engage the broader security and development communities, their impact will be limited. These limitations are well illustrated by recent efforts to formulate a comprehensive plan of action for Somali refugees.

The Somali CPA: attempt at formulating a comprehensive solution

Somalia has been largely neglected by the international community since the withdrawal of US and UN troops between 1994 and 1995. Somalia has one of the lowest human development indexes in the world, and a desperate humanitarian situation. Out of a population of approximately 7m people, some 400,000 are estimated to be internally displaced. Although around 1m refugees have returned in the past decade, most live in conditions of absolute poverty. UN programmes for Somalia are seriously under-funded and UN agencies, such as UNHCR, are forced to base their operations in neighbouring countries, mainly Kenya. The presence of international agencies within Somalia itself is negligible.

In the past two years, however, there has been some renewed international interest in restoring stability within Somalia and initiating a comprehensive solution for the protracted Somali refugee population. The UN Under-Secretary General for Humanitarian Affairs, Jan Egland, visited Somalia in December 2004, the first visit by a high-level UN official to the country in over a decade.

In 2004, UNHCR initiated an international effort to establish a CPA for Somali refugees.[38] This initiative includes most of the major stakeholders including the newly established Somali government, host governments in the region, the European Commission, UNHCR and the co-sponsors of the CPA, Denmark, Netherlands and the UK. The steering group does not include Somaliland or Puntland, two relatively stable regions of Somali that are autonomous, self-governing and, in the case of Somaliland, seeking international recognition as an independent state. With seed funding from the European Commission, the steering group intends to develop a plan of action for presentation to a special inter-governmental meeting for approval and funding, planned for mid-2005.

The effort to create a Somali refugee CPA is seen by UNHCR and some researchers as a test case for solving other protracted refugee situations. Its objectives are to identify appropriate durable solutions for Somali refugees living in the region's host countries, while ensuring that the question of Somali refugees gained prominence on the international agenda. At present, given the continuing instability in southern and central Somalia, the CPA's focus is repatriation to Somaliland and Puntland where conditions for returnees are more secure than in southern and central Somalia. However, for repatriation to be sustained there needs to be increased emphasis on reintegration and post-conflict recovery. Another focus is on possibilities for tapping into development funds to provide stability in areas of return; however, funds for reintegration are limited and donor appeals for Somali repatriation have been seriously under-subscribed. For example, less than half of the $200m for the 2004 Somalia repatriation appeal has been pledged by donor governments so far.

The second objective of the CPA is to examine how human rights and economic conditions for Somali refugees can be improved in host countries, such as Kenya, Ethiopia, Yemen and Djibouti. Local experts are undertaking studies to determine the protection and assistance gaps that need to be addressed in any future projects within the CPA. These studies will form the basis for an action plan that will be presented to donor governments in Geneva in mid-2005, building to a wider donors' conference on Somalia in the autumn 2005. Finally, the European co-sponsors are particularly interested in examining ways to mitigate irregular movements of Somalis to the West, given that Somalis have constituted one of the largest nationalities seeking asylum in Europe over the past decade.

While the plan to establish a Somali refugee CPA is a commendable effort to engage the international donor community in a particularly difficult and complex protracted refugee situation, it does not adequately link humanitarian factors with the underlying and crucially important economic, political and security factors. Finding a solution for resolving the Somali protracted refugee situation requires the restoration of a degree of stability and normality in southern and central Somalia where the security situation has been unstable for well over a decade.

After 13 years of negotiations, the Mbaguthi Peace Process in Nairobi resulted in the November 2004 election of Abdullahi Yusuf Ahmed as the new president of Somalia. The composition of a full cabinet was finally agreed in early 2005. The formation of a new government has not, however, heralded a new era of stability in Somalia. Somaliland does not recognise the new government, and there appears to be substantial opposition from the Islamic courts and rival clans. As a result of this opposition and prevailing instability, the government has not been able to sit in Mogadishu, but remains in Kenya. Proposals for an African Union (AU) stabilisation force to provide security for the new government are contingent upon the return and establishment of the government in Mogadishu, and the probability of such a deployment in the foreseeable future consequently remains slim.

Insecurity remains rife in Somalia, as many leaders of warring factions continue to profit personally from conditions of instability. As a result, most aid agencies have long since pulled out of the country. Intermittent fighting among rival clans in Central and Southern Somalia persists. There are also cases of more targeted violence: in January 2005, the police chief of Mogadishu, who supported the return of the new government and the deployment of a stabilisation force, was murdered in his home.

Instability in Somalia, as with the countries of origin in most protracted refugee situations, underscores the need for a joined-up policy on the part of the international donor community to address the long-standing security implications of chronic refugee populations and humanitarian emergencies. The principal weakness of the Somali refugee CPA is that it remains divorced from the political developments surrounding the return to Mogadishu of the newly elected government. The CPA primarily focuses on repatriation to Somalia and improving conditions in Somalia in order to ensure that refugee returns are sustainable, while making no reference to efforts to establish a lasting peace and effective government.

The lessons from past comprehensive plans of action, such as those in Indochina and Central America, are that humanitarian efforts must be closely linked to political and diplomatic initiatives. Successful CPAs also crucially relied on external political initiatives that preceded and laid the foundations for humanitarian and development programmes. For comprehensive solutions to work, countries of origin need stable central governments – ones which require considerable external support in order for new political roots to take hold. This necessitates not only humanitarian assistance but also security and peacekeeping assistance, including training and equipping police and army as well as assistance targeted at disarming and demobilising warring factions.

Tackling the problem of Somali refugees in Kenya and elsewhere in the region would be a good place to start addressing protracted refugee situations comprehensively. In the Somali case, there are strong security and political reasons for acting now. Unlike other African refugee populations, Somalis have migrated across the world and have established themselves in communities in Europe and North America, creating a pull factor for new groups of Somali emigrants. Perhaps most significantly, for the past 10 years, Somali asylum seekers have been among the top asylum seeking nationalities in Europe. Consequently, several EU governments have sought to find ways both to contain those flows and to return failed asylum seekers, if not directly to Somalia, then to Somaliland or Puntland where conditions are slightly better. Somalia has also been the target of UN arms sanctions which have unsuccessfully tried to curb the flow of small arms from Somalia across the region. Thus, there exist strong incentives for donor governments to support a combined political-humanitarian initiative to resolve the protracted Somali refugee problem.

Framework for a truly comprehensive response

For solutions to be truly comprehensive, and therefore effective, they must involve coordinated engagement from a range of peace and security, development and humanitarian actors. Within the multilateral context, it is important to begin by identifying the full range of actors implicated before specifying the role they should each play. Firstly, from the peace and security sector, sustained engagement is necessary not only from the UN Security Council (UNSC), the Office of the UN Secretary General (UNSG) and the Department of Peacekeeping Operations (DPKO), but also from regional and sub-regional organisations, such as the AU, the Economic Community of West African States (ECOWAS), the South Asian Association for Regional Cooperation (SAARC), Association for Southeast Asian Nations (ASEAN), and foreign and defence ministries in national capitals. Secondly, development actors, from the UN Development Programme (UNDP), the World Bank and international development NGOs to national development agencies, such as DfID and the US Agency for International Development (USAID), would have an important role to play at all stages of a comprehensive solutions. Finally, humanitarian actors, including UNHCR, the UN Office for the Coordination of Humanitarian Activities (UN-OCHA), and the full spectrum of international humanitarian NGOs, need to bring their particular skills and experience to bear.

These three sets of actors will each have individual but related responsibilities in the formulation and implementation of comprehensive solutions for long-standing refugee situations. Central to the success of such an approach will be identifying the causes of the impasses in particular cases and gaining the necessary political support and resources from both donors and regional actors to remove these obstacles. The following framework outlines how such coordinated action could respond to this paper's case studies. The objective of the framework is to outline how to move from impasse to comprehensive plans of action, involving the three durable solutions.

Several protracted refugee situations are currently 'ripe for resolution' through the application of this framework. Progress on various aspects of the stabilisation and consolidation phases of the framework has already been accomplished in Liberia, Burundi and, to a certain extent, Somalia. Each of these cases could be thoroughly reviewed through the optic of a more integrated approach to the formulation and implementation of a comprehensive solution. While more analysis is required to identify the gaps in the current response to each situation, the momentum generated by recent positive developments should not be wasted but used as the

Table 2. **A Framework for Formulating and Implementing Comprehensive Solutions for Protracted Refugee Situations**

	Peace and security (UNSC, UNSG, DPKO, regional organization, foreign and defence ministries)	Development (UNDP, World Bank, NGOs, national development agencies)	Humanitarian (UNHCR, UNICEF, NGOs, UNOCHA)
Analysis phase	Examination of on-going political conflict in country of origin and identify obstacles to resolution of conflict and refugee issue Analysis of impact of protracted refugee situation on host state and regional security	Assessment of the positive and negative impact of the protracted presence of refugees in host states, and assessment of targeted development needs Assessment of reconstruction needs in country of origin	Comprehensive survey of the refugee population, including a demographic analysis of the refugee population Assessment of protection environment and assistance needs in host countries
Consultation phase: Meeting of the three sets of actors to develop a coordinated action plan and establish benchmarks for the three stages of the solution			
Stabilisation phase	Engage in confidence-building measures with host states in the region, countries of origin and major donor state	Targeted development assistance to support local populations (linked with humanitarian actors) Implement programmes to meet basic needs in country of origin	Stabilise the protection environment in the region Stabilise the nutritional and health status of refugees Targeted development assistance to support local populations (linked with development actors) Capacity building of structures and systems in host country
Consultation phase: Meeting between three sets of actors and major stakeholders (including donors, host states and the country of origin) to secure the necessary political will and funding to proceed with solution.			
Consolidation phase	Convene a peace conference with the engagement of donors and principal actors Prepare for necessary peace-keeping deployment.	Implement rehabilitation programmes in refugee populated areas in host countries to encourage local integration	Develop preconditions for the three durable solutions: repatriation, local integration and resettlement
Implementation phase	Implement peace agreement Implement disarmament, demobilisation, reintegration and rehabilitation (DDRR) programmes Implement peacebuilding and institution-building programmes to support transitional government	Implement rehabilitation and reconstruction programmes in the country of origin Work with host countries to ensure the transition from relief to development	Implementation of comprehensive plan of action through the complementary use of the three durable solutions

basis for generating the political will and donor engagement required to realise a truly comprehensive solution.

Aspects of such an integrated approach to addressing refugee situations has been used in the past, especially in a number of operations in Africa. In fact, UNHCR, DPKO and UNDP all have experience of working together. While the effectiveness of such partnerships has sometimes been questionable, as outlined above, it is important to examine why some partnerships have been more successful than others, such as the programmes in the DRC, Guinea, Kenya and Tanzania. More generally, it is important to recognise that a solution cannot truly be comprehensive without the sustained engagement of actors from the security, development and humanitarian sectors. In fact, demonstrating its ability to address long-term refugee problems in a more consistent and comprehensive manner is one way for the UN to demonstrate its relevance and usefulness. In the context of discussions of UN reform,[39] specific consideration should be given to the ability of the proposed Peacebuilding Commission to act as the focus for the planning and implementation of integrated and comprehensive responses to protracted refugee situations.

The success of such an approach will, however, depend entirely on sustained commitment from donor countries and members of the UN Security Council. To this end, such an engagement must be approached as part of a more integrated engagement in the question of refugees. Increased external engagement in regions of refugee origin, comprehensive solutions to protracted refugee situations, and a more holistic approach to ensure effective refugee protection in the regions of origin is the best way to address the significant concerns of Western states, meet the protection needs of refugees, and respond to the concerns of countries of first asylum. Such an approach would ensure effective protection in the region of origin, thereby diminishing the need for individuals to migrate to the West to seek such protection, would be structured around managed comprehensive responses, thereby ensuring the predictability sought by Western states, and would work towards the comprehensive solution of protracted refugee situations, thereby contributing to both the protection of refugees and the legitimate concerns of countries of first asylum.

More generally, there is also an urgent need to identify how the various aspects of a state's foreign, development, assistance, trade and security policies may be harmonised to engage the areas most necessary to promote comprehensive solutions.[40] There is also a need to engage with failed states to restore stability, promote reconstruction, and support effective governance and respect for human rights. And there is a need to engage in failing states to support conflict resolution and management mechanisms, regional approaches to peacekeeping and intervention, and peace negotiations that include consideration for the solution of refugee movements caused by the conflict. There is a need to engage in host states, to ensure refugee self-sufficiency and to recognise refugee populations as important elements of peace negotiations and as stakeholders in the process of reconciliation and reconstruction.

In the long term, governments, individually and collectively, must consider how elements of their external policies and programmes, including trade, aid, development, strategic and diplomatic, may be brought to bear in not only addressing, but preventing refugee flows. Ultimately, it must be recognised that the most efficient, effective and humane approach to refugee situations is their prevention, and states and the UN must finally realise that by engaging the failing and failed states of today that they are preventing the refugee movements of tomorrow.

Acknowledgements

Gil Loescher would like to thank the US Institute for Peace and the Ford Foundation for their support. James Milner would like to thank the Trudeau Foundation for their support. We are also grateful to members of the postgraduate class 'Forced Migration and International Relations' at Oxford for their contributions to our undertanding of protracted refugee situations in Africa and Asia. Some material from this Adelphi Paper appeared in an article, 'The Long Road Home: Protracted Refugee Situations in Africa', published by the authors in *Survival*, Summer 2005, vol. 47, no. 2.

Notes

Introduction

[1] UN High Commission for Refugees (UNHCR), *The State of the World's Refugees: Fifty Years of Humanitarian Action* (Oxford: Oxford University Press, 2000), p. 49.

[2] Mohammed Ayoob, *The Third World Security Predicament: State Making, Regional Conflict and the International System* (Boulder, CO: Lynne Reinner Publishers, 1995).

[3] UNHCR, Executive Committee of the High Commissioner's Programme, 'Economic and Social Impact of Massive Refugee Populations on Host Developing Countries, as well as Other Countries', Standing Committee, 29th Meeting, UN Doc. EC/54/SC/CRP.5, 18 February 2004, p. 2.

[4] Merrill Smith, 'Warehousing Refugees: A Denial of Rights, a Waste of Humanity', *World Refugee Survey 2004* (Washington: US Committee for Refugees, 2004).

[5] Karen Jacobsen, 'Can refugees benefit the state? Refugee resources and African statebuilding', *Journal of Modern African Studies*, vol. 40, no. 4, 2002.

[6] UNHCR, 'Economic and Social Impact of Massive Refugee Populations on Host Developing Countries, as well as Other Countries', p. 3.

Chapter One

[1] For a detailed consideration of some of these issues with particular attention to Africa, see: Jeff Crisp, 'No solutions in sight: the problem of protracted refugee situations in Africa', *New Issues in Refugee Research*, Working Paper No. 75, Geneva: UNHCR, January 2003.

[2] UNHCR, Executive Committee of the High Commissioner's Programme, 'Protracted Refugee Situations', Standing Committee, 30th Meeting, UN Doc. EC/54/SC/CRP.14, 10 June 2004, p. 1.

[3] UNHCR, 'Protracted Refugee Situations', p. 2.

[4] The dynamics of urban protracted refugee situations are more difficult to study because these populations tend not be included in official statistics. Moreover, urban refugees try to minimise their visibility to circumvent government restrictions. It is, however, important not to exclude them from a wider understanding of the political and security implications of long-term refugee popula-

tions as host governments are typically more concerned about foreign populations living in large urban areas, especially in the capital city, than refugees contained in camps on the periphery of the state.

5 UNHCR, 'Protracted Refugee Situations', p. 2.

6 Table 1 includes refugee situations numbering 25,000 or more persons by the end of 2003 which have been in existence for five or more years. Industrialised countries are not included. As numbers are rounded, totals may not add up. The table only includes refugees under the mandate of UNHCR, and therefore does not include the over 4 million Palestinian refugees registered with the United Nations Relief and Works Administration for Palestinian refugees (UNRWA). UNHCR, 'Protracted Refugee Situations'.

7 UNHCR, 'Protracted Refugee Situations', p. 1.

8 Jan Egeland, UN Under-Secretary-General for Humanitarian Affairs, Statement to the UN Security Council, 10 May 2005, reported in IRIN, 'Africa: Too little funding too late may cost millions of lives', 11 May 2005, www.reliefweb.int/rw/rwb.nsf/db900SID/KKEE-6CAR7N?OpenDocument.

9 John Vidal, 'Blacks Need, but Only Whites Receive: Race appears to be skewing the West's approach to aid', *Guardian*, 12 August 1999.

10 UNHCR, *UNHCR Global Report 2001* (Geneva: UNHCR, 2001), p. 137.

11 UNHCR, *UNHCR Global Report 2003* (Geneva: UNHCR, 2003), p. 165.

12 UNHCR, 'Press Release: WFP and UNHCR call for urgent aid for refugees in Africa', 14 February 2003.

Chapter Two

1 Claudena Skran, *Refugees in Inter-war Europe: The Emergence of a Regime* (Oxford: Clarendon Press, 1995).

2 Gil Loescher, *The UNHCR and World Politics: A Perilous Path* (Oxford: Oxford University Press, 2001).

3 Gil Loescher and John Scanlan, *Calculated Kindness: Refugees and America's Half Open Door: 1945 to Present* (New York: The Free Press, 1986).

4 UN Doc. A/41/324, 13 May 1986. See also Luke Lee, 'Toward a World Without Refugees: The United Nations Group of Government Experts on International Cooperation to Avert New Flows of Refugees', *British Yearbook of International Law*, vol. 57 (London: H. Frowde, 1986), pp. 317–336.

5 United Nations, *A more secure world: Our shared responsibility*, Report of the Secretary-General's High-level Panel on Threats, Challenges and Change (New York: United Nations, 2004); and International Commission on Intervention and State Sovereignty, *The Responsibility to Protect* (Ottawa: International Development Research Centre, 2001). For background, see: Christopher Greenwood, 'Is there a right of humanitarian intervention?' *The World Today*, vol. 49, no. 2, February 1993, pp. 34–40; Nigel Rodley (ed.), *To Loose the Band of Wickedness: International Intervention in the Defense of Human Rights* (London: Brasseys, 1992); and Lori Fisler Damrosch (ed.), *Enforcing Restraint: Collective Intervention in Internal Conflicts* (New York: Council on Foreign Relations Press, 1992).

6 This argument is more fully developed in Alan Dowty and Gil Loescher, 'Refugee Flows as Grounds for International Action', *International Security*, vol. 21, no. 1, summer 1996, pp. 43-71.

7 Lori Fisler Damrosch, 'Changing Conceptions of Intervention in International Law', in Laura W. Reed and Carl Kaysen (eds), *Emerging Norms of Justified Intervention* (Cambridge, MA: American Academy of Arts and Sciences, 1993), 100ff.

8   UN Security Council, *UN Security Council Summit Declaration* (New York: United Nations, 1992).

9   Matthew J. Gibney, *The Ethics and Politics of Asylum: Liberal Democracy and the Responses to Refugees* (Cambridge: Cambridge University Press, 2004).

10 Sadako Ogata, *The Turbulent Decade: Confronting the refugee crisis of the 1990s* (New York: W. W. Norton, 2005).

11 For an account of this period see Sadako Ogata, *A Turbulent Decade.*

12 Richard Ullman, 'Redefining Security', *International Security*, Vol. 8, no. 1, summer 1983; Caroline Thomas, *In Search of Security: The Third World in International Relations* (Boulder, CO: Lynne Rienner, 1987); Jessica Matthews, 'Redefining Security', *Foreign Affairs*, vol. 68, no. 2, 1989; Thomas Homer-Dixon, 'On the Threshold: Environmental Changes as Causes of Acute Conflict', *International Security*, vol. 16, no. 2, fall, 1991.

13 Gil Loescher, *Refugee Movements and International Security*, Adelphi Paper 268 (London: Brasseys for the International Institute for Strategic Studies, 1992); Myron Weiner (ed.), *International Migration and Security* (Boulder, CO: Westview Press, 1993).

14 For a critique of this view, see: B. S. Chimni, 'The Global Refugee Problem in the 21st Century and the Emerging Security Paradigm: A Disturbing Trend', in A. Anghie and G. Sturgess (eds), *Legal Visions of the 21st Century: Essays in Honour of Judge Christopher Weermantry* (the Hague: Kluwer Law International, 1998).

15 Aristide R. Zolberg, Astri Suhrke and Sergio Aguayo, *Escape from Violence: Conflict and the Refugee Crisis in the Developing World* (Oxford: Oxford University Press, 1989).

16 Jef Huysmans, 'Migrants as a security problem: dangers of "securitizing" societal issues', in Robert Miles and Dietrich Thränhardt (eds), *Migration and European Integration: The Dynamics of Inclusion and Exclusion* (London: Pinter Publishers, 1995);

Ole Waever, Barry Buzan, Morten Kelstrup and Pierre Lemaitre, *Identity, Migration and the New Security Agenda in Europe* (London: Pinter Publishers, 1993); Ole Waever 'Securitization and Desecuritization', in Ronnie D. Lipshutz, *On Security* (New York: Columbia University Press, 1995); Didier Bigo, 'Securité et immigration', *Cultures et conflits*, 27, 1998; and Dider Bigo, 'Sécurité, immigration et controle social', *Le Monde diplomatique*, October 1996.

17 Joanne van Selm, 'Refugee Protection in Europe and the U.S. after 9/11', in Niklaus Steiner, Mark Gibney and Gil Loescher (eds), *Problems of Protection: The UNHCR, Refugees, and Human Rights* (London: Routledge, 2003); Matthew J. Gibney, 'Security and the ethics of asylum after 11 September', *Forced Migration Review*, 13, 2002; and Aristide Zolberg, 'Guarding the Gates in a World on the Move, http://www.ssrc.org/sept11/essays/zolberg.htm

18 Alice Hills, *Border Security in the Balkans: Europe's Gatekeepers*, Adelphi Paper 371 (Oxford: Oxford University Press for the International Institute for Strategic Studies, 2004).

19 For a critique of proposal to establish regional processing centres, see Gil Loescher and James Milner, 'The missing link: the need for comprehensive engagement in regions of refugee origin', *International Affairs*, vol. 79, no. 3, May 2003, pp. 595–617.

20 Mohammed Ayoob, 'A Subaltern Realist Perspective', in Keith Krause and Michael C. Williams (eds), *Critical Security Studies* (Minneapolis, MN, University of Minnesota Press, 1997), p. 130.

21 Fionna Terry, *Condemned to Repeat? The Paradox of Humanitarian Action* (Ithica, NY: Cornell University Press, 2002); Stephen Stedman and Fred Tanner, *Refugee Manipulation: War, Politics and the Abuse of Human Suffering* (Washington DC: Brookings Institution Press, 2002).

22 Karen Jacobsen, 'A Framework for Exploring the Political and Security Context

of Refugee Populated Areas', *Refugee Survey Quarterly*, vol. 19, no. 1, 2000.

23 UNHCR, 'Economic and Social Impact of Massive Refugee Populations on Host Developing Countries, as well as Other Countries'.

24 Gil Loescher, *Refugee Movements and International Security*.

25 Myron Weiner, *International Migration and Security*, p.16.

26 Macedonian Deputy Foreign Minister, speaking at the Emergency Meeting on the Kosovo Refugee Crisis, Geneva, 6 April 1999.

27 Finn Stepputat, *Refugees, Security and Development. Current Experience and Strategies of Protection and Assistance in 'the Region of Origin'*, Copenhagen: Danish Institute for International Studies, Working Paper No 2004/11, 2004, p. 4.

28 Gil Loescher, *Refugee Movements*, p. 42.

29 *Ibid.*

30 Tiyanjana Maluwa, 'The Refugee Problem and the Quest for Peace and Security in Southern Africa', *International Journal of Refugee Law*, vol. 7, no. 4, 1995, p. 657.

31 *Ibid.*

32 *Ibid.*

32 Bonaventure Rutinwa, 'The end of asylum? The changing nature of refugee policies in Africa', *New Issues in Refugee Research*, Working Paper No. 5, Geneva: UNHCR, May 1999, p. 2.

33 Matthew J. Gibney, 'Security and the ethics of asylum after 11 September'.

33 Bonaventure Rutinwa, 'The Tanzanian Government's Response to the Rwandan Emergency', *Journal of Refugee Studies*, vol. 9, no. 3, 1996, pp. 291– 302.

Chapter Three

1 Benjamin Schiff, *Refugees unto the Third Generation: Aid to the Palestinians* (Syracuse, NY: Syracuse University Press, 1995).

2 Michael Bhatia, 'Repatriation under a Peace Process: Mandated Return in the Western Sahara', *International Journal of Refugee Law*, vol. 15, no. 4, 2003; UNHCR, *State of the World's Refugees: Fifty Years of Humanitarian Action* (Oxford: Oxford University Press, 2000), pp. 266–267.

3 Rosa da Costa, 'Maintaining the Civilian and Humanitarian Character of Asylum', *Legal and Protection Policy Research Series*, Geneva, UNHCR, Department of International Protection, PPLA/2004/02, June 2004.

4 Walter Clarke and Jeffrey Herbst (eds), *Lessons from Somalia: Lessons of armed humanitarian intervention* (Boulder, CO: Westview Press, 1997).

5 UN Security Council Resolution 794, S/RES/794 (1992).

6 UNHCR, *2003 Statistical Yearbook*, p. 211.

7 Jeff Crisp, 'A State of Insecurity: the political economy of violence in refugee-populated areas of Kenya', New Issues in Refugee Research, Working Paper No. 16, Geneva: UNHCR, December 1999; Human Rights Watch, 'Somali Refugees in Kenya' in *The Human Rights Watch Global Report on Women's Human Rights*, (New York: Human Rights Watch, 1995); UNHCR, Inspection and Evaluation Service, 'A review of UNHCR's Women Victims of Violence project in Kenya', Geneva, March 1996.

8 Binaifer Nowrojee and Bronwen Manby, *Divide and Rule: State-sponsored Ethnic Violence in Kenya* (New York: Human Rights Watch, 1993).

9 The Thika Processing Centre, north of Nairobi, was closed in 1994. Three camps around Mombasa (Marafa, Hatimy and Utange), housing almost 83,000 refugees in February 1994, were progressively closed between 1995 and 1998. UNHCR, Branch Office for Kenya, 'Last Coast Province Refugee Camp Closes', UNHCR Press Release, Nairobi, 22 December 1998.

10 There are currently four refugee camps in Kenya. Kakuma Camp, in the northwest

of Kenya and close to the border with Sudan and Uganda, has a population of approximately 71,000 refugees, of whom 80% (56,580 persons) are Sudanese and almost 15% (10,337 persons) are Somalian. There are three refugee camps around Dadaab town in the northeast of Kenya, 80km from the border with Somalia. These camps, Ifo, Dagahaley and Hagadera, together have a population of just over 135,000 refugees, 98% of whom are Somalian. Over 85% of Somali refugees in Kenya live in the Dadaab camps.

[11] Alison Parker, *Hidden in Plain View: Refugees living without protection in Nairobi and Kampala* (New York: Human Rights Watch, 2002).

[12] Monica Kathina Juma and Peter Mwangi Kagwanja, 'Securing Refuge from Terror: Refugee Protection in East Africa after September 11', in Niklaus Steiner, Mark Gibney and Gil Loescher (eds), *Problems of Protection: The UNHCR, Refugees and Human Rights* (New York: Routledge, 2003), pp. 225–236.

[13] Based on interviews conducted in Nairobi in November–December 2001 and March 2004.

[14] BBC News on-line, 'Kenya inquiry targets Somali militants', 30 November 2002.

[15] Danna Harman, 'In a dire Kenyan camp, links to Al Qaeda', *Christian Science Monitor*, 18 December 2002.

[16] Based on interviews conducted in Nairobi in March 2004.

[17] US Department of the Treasury, 'Fact Sheet: Designation of Somalia and Bosnia-Herzegovina Branches of Al-Haramain Islamic Foundation', 11 March 2002.

[18] Integrated Regional Information Network (IRIN), UN Office for the Coordination of International Affairs, 'KENYA: Feature – Making communities safe from small arms', 29 October 2003, www.irinnews.org.

[19] Africa Watch, *Kenya: Taking Liberites* (New York: Africa Watch, July 1991).

[20] UNHCR, Evaluation and Policy Analysis Unit, 'Evaluation of the Dadaab firewood

project, Kenya', Geneva: UNHCR, EPAU/2001/08, June 2001, p. 19.

[21] *Ibid.*

[22] For an overview of these programmes, see Jeff Crisp, 'A State of Insecurity: the political economy of violence in refugee-populated areas of Kenya'.

[23] René Lemarchand and David Martin, 'Selective Genocide in Burundi', Report No. 20, London: The Minority Rights Group, 1974.

[24] Loren Landau, 'The humanitarian hangover: transnationalization of governmental practice in Tanzania's refugee-populated areas', *Refugee Survey Quarterly*, vol. 21, no. 1 and 2, 2002; Beth Elise Whitaker, 'Changing priorities in refugee protection: the Rwandan repatriation from Tanzania', *Refugee Survey Quarterly*, vol. 21, no. 1 and 2, 2002; Sreeram Sundar Chaulia, 'The Politics of Refugee Hosting in Tanzania: From Open Door to Unsustainability, Insecurity, and Receding Receptivity', *Journal of Refugee Studies*, vol. 16, no. 2, 2003.

[25] Louise W. Holborn, *Refugees: A Problem of Our Time: The work of the United Nations High Commissioner for Refugees, 1951–1972*, (Netchen, NJ: The Scarecrow Press, Inc., 1975), pp. 1145–1192.

[26] Charles Gasarasi, *The Tripartite Approach to the Resettlement and Integration of Rural Refugees in Tanzania*, Research report no. 71 (Uppsala: The Scandinavian Institute of African Studies, 1984).

[27] UNHCR, *The State of the World's Refugees: Fifty Years of Humanitarian Action* (Oxford: Oxford University Press, 2000), p. 312.

[28] J. P. Brahim, 'Refugee Crisis in the Great Lakes Region: How Tanzania was affected and her response', paper presented at the International Workshop on Refugee Crisis in the Great Lakes Region, Arusha, 16–19 August 1995.

[29] Bonaventure Rutinwa, 'The Tanzanian Government's Response to the Rwandan Emergency', *Journal of Refugee Studies*, Special Issue, vol. 9, no. 3, 1996.

30 Human Rights Watch, 'In the Name of Security: Forced Round-Ups of Refugees in Tanzania', vol. 11, no. 4, July 1999, p. 1.

31 Khoti Kamanga, 'The (Tanzania) Refugees Act of 1998: Some Legal and Policy Implications', *Journal of Refugee Studies*, vol. 18, no. 1, 2005.

32 International Crisis Group, 'Burundian Refugees in Tanzania: The Key Factor to the Burundian Peace Process', IGC Central Africa Report No. 12, Nairobi: IGC, 30 November 1999.

33 BBC News on-line, 'Tanzania protests Burundi shelling', 4 January 2002.

34 Jeff Crisp, 'Lessons learned from the implementation of the Tanzania security package', Geneva: UNHCR, Evaluation and Policy Analysis Unit, EPAU/2001/05, May 2001; Jean-Francois Durieux, 'Preserving the character of refugee camps: Lessons from the Kigoma refugee programme in Tanzania', *Track Two*, vol. 9, no. 3, November 2000.

35 IRIN, 'Tanzania: President ties rise in small arms to refugee inflows', 1 September 2003, www.irinnews.org.

36 Bonaventure Rutinwa and Khoti Kamanga, 'The Impact of the Presence of Refugees in Northwestern Tanzania', Report by the Centre for the Study of Forced Migration, University of Dar es Salaam, September 2003.

37 Khoti Kamanga, 'The (Tanzania) Refugees Act of 1998: Some Legal and Policy Implications', p. 104.

38 *Ibid.*

39 Greg Collins, 'Coping Strategies Index (CSI) Baseline Survey: World Food Programme (WFP) Assisted Refugees in Western Tanzania', prepared for WFP Tanzania, June–July 2004.

40 US Committee for Refugees (USCR), 'Tanzania', *World Refugee Survey 2000*, Washington: USCR, 2000.

41 US Committee for Refugees (USCR), 'Tanzania', *World Refugee Survey 2001* (Washington: USCR, 2001).

42 IRIN, 'Burundi-Tanzania: IRIN special report on returning Burundian refugees',

8 May 2002. Agencies to have raised concerns about the repatriations include the International Council of Voluntary Agencies, Refugee Council USA, Amnesty International, Refugees International, Human Rights Watch and TCRS. IRIN, 4 April 2002; IRIN, 5 May 2002; IRIN, 15 May 2003; and Refugees International, 'Policy Recommendations: Burundian Refugees in Tanzania: Between a Rock and a Hard Place', 18 June 2003.

43 UNHCR, 'Press Release: New border crossing drums up interest in Burundian return', 24 June 2004.

44 Stephen Ellis, 'Liberia 1989–1994: A Study of Ethnic and Spiritual Violence', *African Affairs*, vol. 94, no. 375, April 1995; Stephen Ellis, 'Liberia's Warlord Insurgency' in Christopher Clapham (ed.), *African Guerrillas* (Oxford: James Currey, 1998); Ibrahim Abdullah and Patrick Muana, 'The Revolutionary United Front of Sierra Leone', in Christopher Clapham (ed.), *African Guerrillas* (Oxford: James Currey, 1998).

45 Refugee population statistics from the Guinea programme have been notoriously problematic since the late 1990s, resulting from a lack of both the necessary training and resources to gather and maintain base-line data, and concerns about corruption. In 2002, the non-governmental US Committee for Refugees reported that 'there is a high level of scepticism and uncertainty about the reliability of the figures on the part of key partners and others' and that many statistics relating to refugee assistance in Guinea were 'tainted by corruption.' USCR, 'Guinea', *World Refugee Survey 2000* (Washington: USCR, 2000).

46 Win van Damme, 'Field Reports: How Liberian and Sierra Leonean Refugees Settled in the Forest Region of Guinea (1990–96)', *Journal of Refugee Studies*, vol. 12, no. 1, 1999.

47 ULIMO was founded in Freetown in Freetown in 1991 from Liberians who had fled the advance of Charles Taylor. The

movement later split into two factions, broadly along ethnic lines. ULIMO-J included mostly Krahns under the leadership of Roosevelt Johnson and was based in Liberia and Côte d'Ivoire. ULIMO-K included mostly Mandingos under the leadership of Alhaji Kromah and based out of southern Guinea. ULIMO was formally disbanded in 1997 under the terms of the Abuja Accords. See: Ellis, 'Liberia's Warlord Insurgency'; and William Reno, *Warlord Politics and African States* (London: Lynne Reinner Publishers, 1998).

48 Tom Kamara, 'Guinea: Confronting Insecurity in the Midst of Unstable Neighbours', WRITENET Paper No. 8/2000, UNHCR, February 2001, p. 3.

49 Lawyers Committee for Human Rights (LCHR), *Refugees, Rebels and the Quest for Justice* (New York: LCHR, 2002), pp. 55–72.

50 USCR, 'Guinea', 2000.

51 Forum on Early Warning and Early Response (FEWER), 'Policy Brief: Guinea-Conakry – Causes and responses to possible conflict,' 19 September 2000.

52 LCHR, *Refugees, Rebels and the Quest for Justice*, p. 74.

53 Amnesty International, 'Guinea and Sierra Leone: No place of refuge', London: AI-Index AFR 05/006/2001, 24 October 2001, p. 3.

54 Human Rights Watch (HRW), 'Liberian Refugees in Guinea: Refoulement, Militarization of Camps and Other Protection Concerns', New York: HRW, vol. 14, no. 8 (A), November 2002.

55 Roy Herrmann, 'Mid-term review of a Canadian security deployment to the UNHCR programme in Guinea', Geneva: UNHCR, Evaluation and Policy Analysis Unit, EPAU/2003/04, October 2003.

56 James Brabazon, *Liberia: Liberians United for Reconciliation and Democracy (LURD)* (London: Royal Institute for International Affairs, February 2003).

57 International Crisis Group, 'Guinée: Incertitudes autout d'une fin de règne', Freetown/Bruxlles: ICG Rapport Afrique

no. 74, 19 December 2003; IRIN, 'Guinea: Economic crisis and Liberian gunmen threaten stability', 15 July 2004.

58 Valerie Sutter, *The Indochinese Refugee Dilemma* (Baton Rouge, LA: Louisiana State Press, 1990).

59 Hazel Lang, *Fear and Sanctuary: Burmese Refugees in Thailand* (Ithaca, NY: Cornell University Southeast Asia Program Publications, 2002); Ananda Rajah, *Burma: Protracted Conflict, Governance and Non-Traditional Security Issues* (Singapore: National University of Singapore, 2002); and Carl Grundy-Warr, 'Forced Migration and Contested Sovereignty Along the Thai-Burma/Myanmar Border', in C. Schofield, D. Newman, A. Drysdale and J.A. Brown (eds), *The Razor's Edge: International Boundaries and Political Geography* (London: Kluwer Law International, 2002), pp. 337–383.

60 Hazel Lang, *Fear and Sanctuary: Burmese Refugees in Thailand*.

61 A newly reconstituted military junta, the State Peace and Development Council (SPDC) replaced SLORC in November 1997.

62 Carl Grundy-Warr, *The Silence and Violence of Forced Migration in Southeast Asia: Overcoming the Walls of Sovereign Indifference*, paper for the International Association for the Study of Forced Migration, Chiang Mai, Thailand, January 2003.

63 Hazel Lang, *Fear and Sanctuary: Burmese Refugees in Thailand*. See also: Human Rights Watch, 'Unwanted and Unprotected: Burmese Refugees in Thailand', New York, 1998.

64 Hazel Lang, *Fear and Sanctuary: Burmese Refugees in Thailand*.

65 Human Rights Watch, 'Out of Sight, Out of Mind: Thai Policy toward Burmese Refugees', New York, 2004.

66 *Ibid.*

67 According to one researcher, by the early 1990s, approximately 35–40 million people had moved as refugees and migrants across national boundaries in

India, Pakistan, Bangladesh, Sri Lanka, Nepal and Bhutan since 1947. Myron Weiner, 'Rejected Peoples and Unwanted Migrants in South Asia,' in Myron Weiner (ed.), *International Migration and Security* (Boulder, CO: Westview Press, 1993), pp. 149–178.

68   Michael Hutt, *Unbecoming Citizens: Culture, Nationhood, and the Flight of Refugees from Bhutan* (New Delhi: Oxford University Press, 2003); Michael Hutt, *Bhutan: Perspectives on Conflict and Dissent* (Gartmore, Scotland: Kiscadale Asia Research Series, No. 4, 1994); Tapan Bose and Rita Manchanda (eds), *States, Citizens and Outsiders: the Uprooted Peoples of South Asia* (Kathmandu: South Asia Forum for Human Rights, 1997); and Leo Rose, *The Politics of Bhutan* (Ithaca, NY: Cornell University Press, 1977).

69   Michael Hutt, *Unbecoming Citizens: Culture, Nationhood, and the Flight of Refugees from Bhutan*, p. 270.

70   Amnesty International, *Bhutan: Human Rights Violations against the Nepali-speaking Population in the South* (London: Amnesty International, 1992); and Amnesty International, *Bhutan: Forcible Exile*, (London: Amnesty International, 1994).

71   Mahendra Lama, *Managing Refugees in South Asia*, Dhaka: Refugee and Migratory Movements Research Unit, Occasional Paper No. 4, 2000.

72   Human Rights Watch, 'Trapped by Inequality: Bhutanese Refugee Women in Nepal', New York, 2003.

73   *The Economist*, 'The horrors in Nepal', 14 April 2005.

74   Amnesty International, 'Nationality, Expulsion, Statelessness and the Right to Return', London, 14 January 2000; Human Rights Watch, 'Nepal: Bhutanese Rfugees Rendered Stateless – Leading Global NGOs Criticize Screening Process', New York, 18 June, 2003; and Human Rights Watch, 'Nepal/Bhutan: Bilateral Talks Fail to Solve Refugee Crisis', New York, 28 October 2003.

75   *Ibid.* See also, Tang Lay Lee, 'Refugees from Bhutan: Nationality, Statelessness and the Right to Return', *International Journal of Refugee Law*, vol. 10, no. 1, 1998.

Chapter Four

1   See, for example: William O'Neill, 'Conflict in West Africa: Dealing with Exclusion and Separation', *International Journal of Refugee Law*, vol. 12, special supplementary issue, 2000; and Bonaventure Rutinwa, 'Screening in mass influxes: the challenge of exclusion and separation', *Forced Migration Review*, no. 13, June 2002.

2   UNHCR, Executive Committee of the High Commissioner's Programme, 'The Security, and Civilian and Humanitarian Character of Refugee Camps and Settlements', Standing Committee, 14th Meeting, UN Doc. EC/49/SC/INF.2, 14 January 1999.

3   Jeff Crisp, 'Lessons Learned from the Implementation of the Tanzania Security Package', Geneva: UNHCR, Evaluation and Policy Analysis Unit, EPAU/2001/05, May 2001.

4   Lisa Yu, *Separating Ex-Combatants and Refugees in Congo, DRC: Peacekeepers and UNHCR's 'Ladder of Options'*, New Issues in Refugee Research, Working Paper No. 60 (Geneva, UNHCR, August 2002).

5   Mats Berdal, 'The UN After Iraq', *Survival*, vol. 46, no. 3, 2004, pp. 83–102. Berdal cites Kofi Annan's May 2004 speech outlining for the Security Council the multidimensional tasks of today's peace-keeping missions: 'Peacekeeping today has become increasingly multidimen-sional. The missions you mandate are implementing peace agreements, help-ing manage political transition, building institutions, supporting economic reconstruction, organising the return of refugees and internally displaced persons, assisting humanitarian aid programmes,

supervising or even organising elections, monitoring human rights, clearing minefields, disarming and demobilising militias, and reintegrating their members into the civilian economy'.

6 Mats Berdal, 'The UN After Iraq'.

7 Karen Jacobsen, 'Can refugees benefit the state? Refugee resources and African statebuilding', *Journal of Modern African Studies*, vol. 40, no. 4, 2002.

8 Information for this section is drawn from CARE Kenya and UNHCR programme documents and interviews with programme staff in Dadaab, Kenya, March 2004.

9 UNHCR, 'Protracted Refugee Situations', UNHCR, Standing Committee, 30th Meeting, 10 June 2004, EC/54/SC/CRP.14.

10 Yéfime Zarjevski, *A Future Preserved: International Assistance to Refugees* (Oxford: Pergamon Press for the Office of the United Nations High Commissioner for Refugees, 1988) pp. 88–90 and Gil Loescher, *The UNHCR and World Politics: A Perilous Path* (Oxford: Oxford University Press, 2001), pp. 89–91.

11 Statement by the UN High Commissioner for Refugees at Meeting of American Immigration Conference, 28 October 1958, UNHCR Archives HCR/1/7/5/USA/CAN.

12 UNHCR, *State of the World's Refugees*, 2000, p. 84.

13 UNHCR, 'International Conference on Indo-Chinese Refugees: Report of the Secretary General [Annex: Declaration and Comprehensive Plan of Action (CPA)]', 1989.

14 The CPA has been criticised for a number of reasons. Shamsul Bari, 'Refugee Status Determination under the Comprehensive Plan of Action (CPA): A Personal Assessment', *International Journal of Refugee Law*, vol. 4, no. 4, 1992; W. Courtland Robinson, *Terms of Refuge: The Indochinese Exodus and the International Response* (London: Zed Books, 1998); Astri Shurke, 'Burden Sharing during Refugee Emergencies: The Logic of Collective versus National Action', *Journal of Refugee Studies*, vol. 11, no. 4, 1998.

15 UNHCR, 'International Conference on Central American Refugees: Report to the Secretary General', 1989, and UNHCR, 'Comprehensive and regional approaches to refugee problems', EC/1994/SCP/CRP.3, 3 May 1994.

16 UNHCR, Executive Committee of the High Commissioner's Programme, 'Agenda for Protection', Fifty-third session, UN Doc. Ac.96/965/Add.1, 26 June 2002, Preamble, Goal 5.

17 Karen Jacobsen, 'The Forgotten Solution: Local integration for refugees in developing countries', *New Issues in Refugee Research*, Working Paper No. 45 (Geneva: UNHCR, July 2001).

18 UNHCR, 'Agenda for Protection', Preamble, Goal 5.

19 Alexander Betts, 'International Cooperation and the Targeting of Development Assistance for Refugee Solutions: Lessons from the 1980s', *New Issues in Refugee Research*, Working Paper no. 107 (Geneva: UNHCR, September 2004); Barry N. Stein, 'ICARA II: Burden Sharing and Durable Solutions' in John R. Rogge (ed.), *Refugees: A Third World Dilemma* (Totowa, NJ: Rowman and Littlefield Publishers, 1987).

20 UNHCR, Executive Committee of the High Commissioner's Programme, 'The Strategic Use of Resettlement', Standing Committee, 27th Meeting, UN Doc. EC/53/SC/CRP.10/Add.1, 3 June 2003.

21 UNHCR, 'Strengthening and Expanding Resettlement Today: Dilemmas, Challenges and Opportunities', Global Consultations on International Protection, 4th Meeting, EC/GC/02/7, 25 April 2002.

22 European Council on Refugees and Exiles (ECRE) and US Committee for Refugees (USCR), *Responding to the Asylum and Access Challenge: An Agenda for Comprehensive Engagement in Protracted Refugee Situations*, USCR and ECRE, August 2003, pp. 37–42.

23 On the prospects of a European resettlement programme, see: European Council on Refugees and Exiles (ECRE), 'Towards a European Resettlement Programme', *The Way Forward: Europe's role in the global refugee protection system*, London: ECRE, 2005, http://www.ecre.org/positions/wfres.pdf

24 B.S. Chimni, *From resettlement to involuntary repatriation: A critical history of durable solutions to refugee problems*, New Issues in Refugee Research, Working Paper No. 2, UNHCR, May 1999, and Michael Barutciski, 'Developments: Involuntary Repatriation when Refugee Protection is no longer Necessary: Moving forward after the 48th Session of the Executive Committee', *International Journal of Refugee Law*, vol. 10, no. 1/2, 1998.

25 UNHCR, 'Briefing Notes: High Commissioner's Forum', 27 June 2003; Ruud Lubbers, UN High Commissioner for Refugees, 'Opening Statement at the First Meeting of the High Commissioner's Forum', Geneva, 27 June 2003; UNHCR, 'Background Document: Initiatives that could benefit from Convention Plus', High Commissioner's Forum, Forum/2003/03, 18 June 2003.

26 Larry Minear and Iain Smillie, *The Quality of Money: Donor Behavior in Humanitarian Financing* (Somerville, MA: Humanitarianism and War Project, Tufts University, April 2003).

27 The Refugee Policy Group in Washington DC produced reports on protracted refuge settlements in Africa outlining many of the problems confronting long-staying refugees at that time. T. Betts, Robert Chambers and Art Hansen, among others, conducted research on some of these groups in Africa and assessed the international community's policy responses, particularly programs aimed to promote local integration.

28 Individual studies conducted for the research are posted on the web-page of UNHCR's Evaluation and Policy Analysis Unit: http://www.unhcr.ch/epau. For a summary of the research findings, see Jeff Crisp, 'No solutions in sight: the problem of protracted refugee situations in Africa', Paper prepared for a symposium on the multidimensionality of displacement in Africa, held in Kyoto, Japan, November 2002.

29 UNHCR Africa Bureau, 'Discussion Paper on Protracted Refugee Situations in the African Region', Background paper prepared for the 52nd Session of UNHCR's Executive Committee, October 2001; UNHCR's Africa Bureau, 'Informal Consultations: New Approaches and Partnerships for Protection and Solutions in Africa', December 2001; and UNHCR, 'Chairman's Summary: Informal Consultations on New Approaches and Partnerships for Protection and Solutions in Africa', December 2001. Papers available on-line at: http://www.unhcr.ch

30 Ruud Lubbers, UN High Commissioner for Refugees, 'Opening Statement to the 53rd Session of the Executive Committee of the High Commissioner's Programme', Geneva, 30 September 2002.

31 UNHCR, Executive Committee of the High Commissioner's Programme, 'Agenda for Protection', Standing Committee, 24th Meeting, UN Doc. EC/52/SC/CRP.9, 11 June 2002.

32 UNHCR, 'Briefing Notes: High Commissioner's Forum', 27 June 2003; Ruud Lubbers, UN High Commissioner for Refugees, 'Opening Statement at the First Meeting of the High Commissioner's Forum', Geneva, 27 June 2003; UNHCR, 'Background Document: Initiatives that could benefit from Convention Plus', High Commissioner's Forum, Forum/2003/03, 18 June 2003.

33 Karen Jacobsen, 'Can refugees benefit the state? Refugee resources and African statebuilding', *Journal of Modern African Studies*, vol. 40, no. 4, 2002.

34 Oliver Bakewell, 'Repatriation and Self-Settled Refugees in Zambia: Bringing Solutions to the Wrong Problems', *Journal of Refugee Studies*, vol. 13, no. 4, December 2000.

[35] Alexander Betts, 'International cooperation and the targeting of development assistance for refugee solutions: Lessons from the 1980s', *New Issues in Refugee Research*, UNHCR Working Paper no. 107, Geneva, September 2004.

[36] UNHCR, Executive Committee of the High Commissioner's Programme, 'Protracted Refugee Situations', Standing Committee, 30th Meeting, UN Doc. EC/54/SC/CRP.14, 10 June 2004, p. 4.

[37] UNHCR, High Commissioner's Forum, 'Making Comprehensive Approaches to Resolving Refugee Problems more Systematic', UN Doc. FORUM/2004/7, 16 September 2004.

[38] This section on the Somalia CPA is based upon authors' interviews with staff of UNHCR Africa Bureau, Geneva, September 2004.

[39] United Nations, *A more secure world: Our shared responsibility: Report of the High Level Panel on Threats, Challenges and Change*, (New York: United Nations, 2004).

[40] Oxfam, *Foreign Territory: The Internationalisation of EU Asylum Policy*, (Oxford: Oxfam, May 2005); Gil Loescher and James Milner, 'The Missing Link: The Need for Comprehensive Engagement in Regions of Refugee Origin', *International Affairs*, vol. 79, no. 3, 2003.